T0318612

Cambridge Elements ≡

Elements in Critical Heritage Studies
edited by
Kristian Kristiansen, *University of Gothenburg*
Michael Rowlands, *UCL*
Francis Nyamnjoh, *University of Cape Town*
Astrid Swenson, *Bath University*
Shu-Li Wang, *Academia Sinica*
Ola Wetterberg, *University of Gothenburg*

HERITAGE TOURISM

From Problems to Possibilities

Yujie Zhu
Australian National University

CAMBRIDGE
UNIVERSITY PRESS

CAMBRIDGE
UNIVERSITY PRESS

University Printing House, Cambridge CB2 8BS, United Kingdom

One Liberty Plaza, 20th Floor, New York, NY 10006, USA

477 Williamstown Road, Port Melbourne, VIC 3207, Australia

314–321, 3rd Floor, Plot 3, Splendor Forum, Jasola District Centre,
New Delhi – 110025, India

79 Anson Road, #06–04/06, Singapore 079906

Cambridge University Press is part of the University of Cambridge.

It furthers the University's mission by disseminating knowledge in the pursuit of
education, learning, and research at the highest international levels of excellence.

www.cambridge.org
Information on this title: www.cambridge.org/9781108823395
DOI: 10.1017/9781108914024

© Yujie Zhu 2021

First published 2021

A catalogue record for this publication is available from the British Library.

ISBN 978-1-108-82339-5 Paperback
ISSN 2632-7074 (online)
ISSN 2632-7066 (print)

Heritage Tourism

From Problems to Possibilities

Elements in Critical Heritage Studies

DOI: 10.1017/9781108914024
First published online: May 2021

Yujie Zhu
Australian National University

Author for correspondence: Yujie Zhu, yujie.zhu@anu.edu.au

Abstract: As one of the world's fastest-growing industries, heritage tourism is surrounded by political and ethical issues. This research explores the social and political effects and implications of heritage tourism through several pertinent topics. It examines the hegemonic power of heritage tourism and its consequences, the spectre of nationalism and colonialism in heritage-making, particularly for minorities and indigenous peoples, and the paradox of heritage tourism's role in combatting these issues. Drawing from global cases, the study addresses a range of approaches and the challenges of empowerment within the context of heritage tourism, including cultural landscapes, intangible heritage and ecomuseums. The research argues that heritage tourism has the potential to develop as a form of co-production. It can be used to create a mechanism for community-centred governance that integrates recognition and interpretation and promotes dialogue, equity and diversity.

Keywords: politics, empowerment, heritage, tourism, community

ISBNs: 9781108823395 (PB), 9781108914024 (OC)
ISSNs: 2632-7074 (online), 2632-7066 (print)

Contents

1 Introduction

In my travels, I have often visited a town called Lijiang in the south-west of China, not far from Laos, Burma and Vietnam. Like me, millions of tourists from all over the world visit the place, fascinated by its mountain scenery, narrow waterways, traditional architecture and unique ethnic minority culture. After the United Nations Educational, Scientific and Cultural Organization (UNESCO) listed Lijiang as a World Heritage Site in 1997, the rapidly growing heritage tourism industry has had a tremendous impact on the social fabric of the town. Heritage tourism has created employment opportunities and provided resources for building restoration and cultural revitalisation. At the same time, the original residents of the town have developed a collective sense of displacement due to spatial transformation, rising living costs and increased commercialisation.

These tourism impacts are representative of the global tourism industry's response to significant changes resulting from global interconnectedness (Timothy and Boyd 2006). As in Lijiang, the conversion of cultural and natural resources into tourism sites and commodities is fuelled by both the private and public sectors' economic interests. The tourism industry generates billions of dollars for the global economy each year. It encompasses an array of fiscal revenues, including employment, site visitation fees, transport, food, accommodation and souvenirs (Timothy and Boyd 2003). Within this context, heritage tourism is one of the fastest-growing aspects of the tourism industry, employing millions of people directly and indirectly.

While the benefits can be substantial, the negative features of this rapid growth and adoption of heritage for tourism purposes can be significant. For Lijiang and numerous other sites around the world, heritage can become used for un(intended) purposes. What concepts and approaches are useful for understanding this global phenomenon? How does global tourism consumption shape the interpretation and presentation of cultural heritage? And how can different stakeholders use heritage tourism to ensure a more sustainable future?

This research examines the key political and ethical issues that emerge through heritage tourism as one of the fastest-growing niches of the global tourism industry. It provides critical analysis to explain the multifaceted relationship between heritage and tourism. This approach is situated in the development of critical heritage studies and critical tourism studies, two interdisciplinary fields of academic study that have developed in recent decades.

Drawing from cases all around the world, I address a range of existing approaches and the challenges of empowerment and sustainable development within the heritage tourism context. Heritage tourism should not be taken simply as an economic and management business, but instead should be seen as a global

Figure 1 Mass tourism in Lijiang, China

political and ethical project associated with the power of dominant actors and the hopes of the marginalised. Furthermore, this research seeks to provide a critical account of how communities, international organisations and national and local governments manage heritage tourism as an exercise of co-production. In so doing, heritage tourism can be developed as a social movement to empower dialogue, equity and diversity. These issues become particularly relevant and essential today with the rise of deglobalisation and nationalism.

Definitions: Heritage, Tourism and Heritage Tourism

Defining heritage tourism is not an easy task. Both terms ('heritage' and 'tourism') are value-laden concepts explored by all sorts of disciplines, including sociology, anthropology, history, geography, cultural studies, political science and management. Each of them brings particular research methods and theories to study heritage and tourism as separate but sometimes interrelated subjects.

Traditionally, heritage refers to cultural performances, buildings and objects representing an 'authentic' past or environment. In the past decades, scholars have called for a shift in the understanding of heritage from conservation of the past to the politics of the past (Tunbridge and Ashworth 1996; Harrison 2013; Lähdesmäki, Thomas and Zhu 2019). Instead of defining heritage in terms of material objects, recent scholarship sees heritage as a cultural, economic and political resource (Tunbridge and Ashworth 1996), a discursive practice (Smith 2006) and a process of acts that engage with the past, present and future (Harvey 2001).

Many scholars have argued for a broadly 'presentist' approach when engaging with heritage (Tunbridge and Ashworth 1996; Harvey 2001). As Tunbridge and Ashworth (1996) note, 'the present selects an inheritance from an imagined past for current use and decides what should be passed on to an imagined future' (6). This statement indicates the complexities of heritage: it is produced in the present for and about our everyday experiences.

While many forms of heritage exist, such as cultural, natural or 'mixed' (both cultural and natural heritage), this research focuses mostly on cultural heritage in both tangible and intangible forms.[1] It includes various material objects associated with historic buildings, monuments, archaeological ruins and museums, or movable objects such as antique collections, handicrafts and arts. Conversely, cultural heritage can also include non-material elements such as music, rituals, festivals, foodways and folklores.

I use the United Nations World Tourism Organization's (UNWTO) (2008) definition of tourism as a 'social, cultural and economic phenomenon which entails the movement of people to countries or places outside their usual environment for personal or business/professional purpose'. Here three key elements exist in the various definitions. Tourism can refer to the human desire to know others and ourselves, an action for people to move away from a known habitat and stay somewhere else, or various sorts of consumption of goods, services and experiences of place (Leiper 1979; Garrod and Fyall 2001).

For this research, heritage tourism is defined as tourism experiences related to or derived from historical sites or practices. Broadly, heritage tourism concerns cultural, ethnic and historical aspects of the past that attract tourists and travellers (Chang 1999). As 'heritage and tourism are collaborative industries, heritage [converts] locations into destinations' (Kirshenblatt-Gimblett 1998, 151). In other words, heritage is the use of the past for present sociocultural purposes of tourism (Timothy and Boyd 2003; Palmer and Tivers 2019). Often the term 'heritage tourism' is a marketing device used by tourism operators who create different products that refer to historic towns, archaeological ruins, ancient monuments, religious sites and living culture (Salazar and Zhu 2015, 241).

Critical Approaches in Heritage Tourism

This research is mainly embedded in the critical turn in tourism and heritage studies since the 1990s. This period draws on the earlier movements of post-war recovery in the 1950s, 1960s and 1970s, which saw the development of tourism industries as a business management strategy to increase profitability. Some

---

[1] I admit that culture and nature, tangible and intangible should not be treated as simple separate dichotomies. These definitions are used only for this research.

early research in tourism studies during the 1960s and 1970s focused on the business and management of the tourism industry, while the 'negative' perceptions of the sociocultural dimension were ignored (Xiao, Jafari, Cloke and Tribe 2013). Such scholarship was embedded in a professional discourse that legitimised and promoted efficiency, competition and entrepreneurship (Ball 2013). As a result, a large body of literature has been produced regarding policy and industry-based research, including topics on sustainability, technology and carrying capacity (Morgan, Pritchard, Causevic and Minnaert 2018). Influenced by positivist and quantitative approaches, such management-oriented research often focused on product development, strategic marketing, destination images and tourist satisfaction.

Since the late 1960s, a division has been created in academia between tourism as a field of management and tourism as a field of social studies (Tribe 2007). The latter concerns the social, cultural and political perspectives of the tourism industry. Anthropologist Theron Nuñez (1963) studied the interrelation between tourists and local communities by focusing on weekend travel in a Mexican peasant village. His work 'Tourism, Tradition, and Acculturation: *Weekendismo* in a Mexican Village' is often credited as one of the earliest tourism-related articles in American anthropological literature.

Since the 1970s, interest in the social and cultural aspects of tourism has proliferated exponentially. To capture these research interests and developments, whilst supplementing a gap in published material, the *Annals of Tourism Research* was established in 1973 as one of the earliest journals to engage with tourism as a field of social science. Along with the publication of the seminal work *Hosts and Guests* in 1977, sociologists and anthropologists such as Valene Smith, Nelson Graburn, Erick Cohen and Eduard Bruner set a precedent in tourism studies by considering the relationship between tourism and society. While some of them, such as Dennison Nash (1978), proposed tourism as a form of postcolonial imperialism, others viewed tourism as a social and ritualistic practice (see Graburn 1983). Using Foucault's work on the 'gaze', John Urry (1990) illustrated the asymmetrical power relationship between tourists and hosts. Crang (1997) further argued that the study of the tourism industry should not be disconnected from the broader economic and political context where it is situated. A large amount of new scholarship has since been developed along with wider sociological and anthropological thoughts and theories such as embodiment, performance, gender, non-representation, postcolonialism, cosmopolitanism and mobilities.

Since 2000, a further critical approach has been developed to engage the tourism industry, phrased as critical tourism studies (CTS). This trend was witnessed by the establishment of the journals *Tourist Studies* in 2000 and

Tourism and Cultural Change in 2003, and by the organisation of the first Critical Tourism Studies Conference by Ateljevic, Pritchard and Morgan in Dubrovnik, Croatia, in 2005. These newly established journals and association meetings provided platforms to develop critical scholarship of tourism as a social phenomenon.

The ideas of CTS were influenced by the philosophical and sociological legacies of the Frankfurt school. Arising out of the failure of the left-wing class movement and the rise of fascism and capitalist markets, the Frankfurt school was founded at the Institute for Social Research at Goethe University, Frankfurt, during the Weimar Republic (1918–33). Along with the intellectual contribution by scholars such as Horkheimer, Adorno, Marcuse and Habermas, the Frankfurt school criticised contemporary capitalism and rejected the positivist dichotomy between fact and value, theory and politics (Best and Kellner 1997, 223). Further, they illustrated the limitation of existing social theories such as Marxism due to positivism, materialism and determinism; instead, they established components of alternative social theory that search for the political, economic and societal conditions for social emancipation.

As John Tribe (2007) summarised, CTS is a critique of the existing positivist, managerial paradigm that is still dominant in some tourism studies literature. With support from the post-structuralist, humanistic, neo-Marxist, critical realist, feminist and postmodern approaches, CTS intends to jump out of the hegemonic trap of tourism that is deeply embedded in Western capitalism and consumerism (Hall 2013; Morgan et al. 2018). Subsequently, the critical turn of tourism studies focuses on 'the forces of domination, hegemony and alienation, the practice and particulars of lived experience, the values and beliefs of the marginalised and unrecognised, and the potential for emancipation' (Bramwell and Lane 2014, 1).

Following the recent critical turn in tourism studies, I identify two research agendas of the critical approaches to studying heritage tourism. The first approach brings Foucauldian thought to challenge hegemonic power in the formation of knowledge production in heritage tourism (Tribe 2007). Recently, there has been a 'discursive turn' in heritage studies that pays close attention to the knowledge effects of heritage and its impact on societies and people. The political work heritage does is particularly evident in heritage policies and institutions that are rooted in discourses dominated by the West (Winter 2014). Using the term *les lieux de mémoire* (sites of memory), Pierre Nora (1989) indicated that the promotion of national history and sites of memory facilitates the development of a collective national memory that homogenises local memories in France. Heritage professionals and experts often participate in the constitution of what Laurajane Smith (2006) has called an 'authorised heritage discourse' – a discourse that 'not only organises the way concepts like heritage are understood, but the ways we act, the social and technical practices we act out, and the way knowledge is constructed and reproduced' (4). As a result, heritage professionals and experts institutionalise their methods of evaluating heritage through state actors, which creates a hegemonic discourse and understanding of heritage (Smith 2006). This discussion focuses not only on the rights of access to knowledge, but also on the power of knowledge production and its impacts on how heritage is managed, presented and understood (Harrison 2013, 109).

This research identifies the power differentials, the central sources and structural marginalisation of certain segments within the heritage tourism context. The critical approach of studying heritage tourism rejects the economic determinism and agendas inherent in structuralism. Instead, it deals with 'the relationship between [tourism] discourses and the diverse forms of capitalist development and territorial logic of state power' (Bianchi 2009, 493). In *Justice and Ethics in Tourism*, Tazim Jamal (2019) explores key issues of tourism ethics, including capacity building, recognition and democracy. Subsequently, heritage tourism is associated not only with consumption and management, but also with various moral and ethical issues such as social inequality, dominance, civil rights and human justice (Jamal 2019). Questions include, but are not limited to, whether heritage tourism legitimates power domination and control or whether it facilitates recognising the rights and needs of different social groups.

The second critical approach of studying heritage tourism calls for de-essentialisation, pluralisation, and emancipation. As Tunbridge and Ashworth (1996) argue, all heritage is dissonant and shaped by different opinions and interpretations. Critical studies of heritage tourism consider power in multiple forms and not just in the hands of elites (Tribe 2008). It empowers actors that have been marginalised in the tourism discourse. It respects different forms of cultural interpretation and meanings of the knowledge system, while considering the social context behind those processes.

In the article 'The Critical Turn and Its Implications for Sustainable Tourism Research', Bramwell and Lane (2014) summarise several essential features of CTS, with the keywords of 'empowerment' and 'emancipation'. Here, the idea of emancipation is not about radical social movements, but concerns the way liberalisation and autonomy work to combat constraints on human identity and agency (Bramwell and Lane 2014). In this sense, emancipation seeks out agents for 'dialogue, reflexivity, equality, empowerment and co-created knowledge' (Pritchard and Morgan 2007, 26).

Following these research agendas, this research calls for a critical and more democratic approach to heritage tourism. It examines the relationship between international organisations, states and experts (usually the providers of know-ledge) and local communities (usually the recipients of knowledge). A key concern is, therefore, the empowerment of local communities to engage with heritage tourism and how their engagement is linked to their well-being and cultural identity (Affleck and Kvan 2008).

In particular, heritage tourism dynamics refers to the power relation between the local and the global, especially within the context of recognition and repre-sentation of indigenous communities within a nation (Theodossopoulos 2013). Hollinshead (1992) asks how it is possible to escape from the discourse of ethnocentric Western portrayals of indigenous North Americans. Does tourism still serve as a powerful instrument for postcolonial imperialism? Or does tourism function as a mechanism of decolonisation and empowerment through self-knowledge and self-governance based upon communities' determinations (Bunten and Graburn 2018, 249)? Further, can tourism offer indigenous people new avenues to 'reach out to the world in search of new allies and supportive connections' and develop self-awareness and cultural identity (Theodossopoulos 2018, 99)?

There are no simple answers to the questions of both research agendas, as they go back to the debates of power and agency. However, the key issue here is that critical approaches to heritage tourism do not limit themselves to critiquing economic, political and sociocultural tourism-related issues. Instead, they encourage transformations and changes that could improve social justice, which often occurs alongside other social movements such as the civil rights, Black Lives Matter and Me Too movements (Jamal 2019).

Outline

Instead of asking how we can better manage heritage tourism, this research examines what heritage tourism does to societies and the ways heritage tourism can be developed for a better future. This research considers several pertinent topics in this area: the hegemonic power of global systems in heritage tourism and its consequences, the spectre of nationalism and colonialism in heritage-making, particularly for minorities and indigenous people, and the paradox of heritage tourism's role in combatting these issues.

After introducing a brief history of heritage tourism in Section 2, I provide an intellectual background on the impact of global tourism on heritage sites and their associated communities. Section 3 investigates the politics of heritage tourism and its influence on our everyday lives. Power is a central issue here, as heritage tourism is not merely a modern form of consumption; instead, it should be treated as a political, social and cultural discourse situated in the postcolonial and globalisation context. As Western ideologies provide a global system of values and beliefs, heritage tourism becomes a channel to appropriate these ideologies in other regions of the world. The global industry facilitates the establishment of social relations and practices that legitimise the ways we understand the world and our past.

Discovering the power relations and the influences of Western ideologies on societies is only the first step in unpacking these issues. In Section 4, I further explore how individuals and social groups increase their capacity to determine their values and belief systems in the heritage tourism industry. This section focuses on helping local communities exert control over social, economic and political factors that affect their lives in the heritage tourism industry. Through various ways of recognising local culture, such as cultural landscapes, intangible heritage and ecomuseums, heritage tourism can be used as a tool to empower local communities for social cohesion and well-being. However, the actual practices do not always serve the needs for emancipation. The challenges of policy implementation are still situated in the existing asymmetrical relationship between those in/with authority and those without.

In Section 5, I seek out possible ways to achieve emancipation by suggesting an approach to heritage tourism that I refer to as 'co-production': a community-centred mechanism of collaborative work associated with planning, design and management. Here, the idea of co-production should not be another marketing cliché or cultural policy driven by international organisations. By examining the mechanisms of local collaborative governance, recognition and heritage interpretation, I illustrate that heritage tourism should be based on dialogical principles linking researchers, planners and communities on the local scale. The success of co-production is not only associated with sufficient funding and management resources, but also relies on local social capital such as trust, empathy and social resilience.

As shown in the concluding section, this research offers broader implications for the ways we engage with critical global issues in the humanities and social sciences. It seeks to illustrate some navigational markers for studying heritage tourism, especially in the context of new challenges and trends in the world such as the emergence of online media and new technologies, mass migrations and displacement through exile, and the global climate and pandemic crises. The field of heritage tourism is vast, and this research cannot cover all the challenges. I intend to avoid a Western-dominated view by opening an inclusive conversation and sharing stories and cases from all around the world. I also hope to offer some useful insights or provide a starting point for pluralistic, dialectical and reflective conversations around the future of heritage and tourism studies.

Now let us begin with a journey into the history of heritage tourism.

2 A Brief History

Although mass tourism to heritage sites is a modern phenomenon, the inter-action between people and their past can be traced back to much earlier times. Romans were interested in and visited the ruins of Greece to embrace their ancient spirit (Lowenthal 2015). Chinese literati and scholars travelled to mountains and forests to pursue spiritual self-nourishment in the Imperial era.

Researchers offer various explanations of the roots of heritage tourism in Europe. Some scholars believe heritage tourism might have originated from pilgrimage in the medieval period as a way of 'discovering the world' (Light 2015). An example of medieval literature describing such pilgrimage activities, albeit in a narrative frame, is Chaucer's *The Canterbury Tales* (1387–1400). Within this narrative, Chaucer described pilgrims' motivations for travelling as a mixture of religious and spiritual movements to Canterbury Cathedral, along with drinking, sex and merrymaking (Franklin 2003).

Heritage tourism in Europe can also be traced back to the grand tour of wealthy European elites in the seventeenth century. In this period, the children of aristocrats and gentry were sent on an extended tour of Europe to visit the remains of antiquity, explore cosmopolitan centres abroad and make politically important contacts. In addition to diplomatic and military excursions, the grand tour is the earliest example of cultural – as opposed to religious or spiritual – tours in Europe (Timothy 2011, 3). The travel itinerary often included Western Europe via Paris, Milan, Venice, Florence and Rome and then a return to the UK (Towner 1985, 301). These tours mainly served educational purposes: travellers would learn European languages, art, history and architecture while enjoying the scenery. The tour was regarded as a mark of prestige, a way for youths to testify to their families that they were grown up and a foundation for their cosmopolitan professions. Such educational trips were often costly; therefore, they were exclusive to members of the European upper middle class.

Like in Europe, early travel activities in Asia did not only involve religious pilgrimages derived from Hinduism, Buddhism and other ancient philosophies, but also included government or diplomatic affairs. In Imperial China (221 BC–AD 1912), emperors often went on journeys to inspect their land while officials conducted essential missions. Emperor Taizong dispatched the Buddhist monk Xuan Zang (602–64) to India to collect religious books. Similarly, the Chinese explorer and diplomat Zheng He (1371–1433) was sent by Emperor Yongle around Asia and Africa during the early fifteenth century. Chinese literati often wrote poems about their official and personal journeys visiting temples and climbing mountains with family and friends (Nyíri 2006). Others travelled to natural areas to conduct scientific research or escape from political control.

These travels were influenced by Chinese philosophy, especially the ideas of Taoism that emphasised travel as the best way to engage with nature.

Similar to Imperial China, early travel in Japan was populated by officials, literati and intellectuals. Diplomatic and trade travel can be traced back to the seventh century when the imperial Japanese court sent royal family members (*kuge*) and monks to China, Korea and India to advance their culture, economy and science. In 1643, a well-known neo-Confucian philosopher and writer, Hayashi Gahō, published an early form of travel guide, *Three Views of Japan*. The book described Japan's most scenic historical areas, including Itsukushima, which was listed as a UNESCO World Heritage Site in 1996. Following in Hayashi Gahō's footsteps, forty years later, another poet, Matsuo Bashō, travelled to the far north of Japan and wrote one of the most significant texts of Japanese literature, *Oku no Hosomichi* (*The Narrow Road to the Deep North*). Early forms of tourism in Japan, especially in the Edo period (1603–1868), were almost exclusively confined to the Japanese islands due to isolationist policies. Following the Meiji Reform (1868–1912), the country gradually opened up to foreigners, enabling more accessible and flexible travel conditions.

The Industrial Revolution coming out of the UK in the early nineteenth century played a significant role in shaping the landscape for travelling. On one hand, people treated rapid industrialisation as a threat to civilisation that led to a certain degree of heritage or memory 'crisis'. Efforts to consolidate and record threatened civilisations, cultural groups and assets became a priority. On the other hand, the invention of ships, steam trains and photography and the establishment of rail networks stimulated travel among members of the middle class.

In 1846, the German publisher Karl Baedeker (1801–59) introduced the star rating system in his travel handbooks to evaluate tourism destinations. The Verlag Karl Baedeker later became a pioneer in travel literature and one of the most successful travel guide publishing houses in the world. Nineteen years later, in 1865, the English businessman Thomas Cook established one of the first tourism agencies and started the era of package tourism.[2] As the father of modern travel agents and tour operations, Cook offered ship- and train-based tours, testing his programme first in Italy and later expanding to Europe. The itineraries of his packaged tours were mainly heritage-based such as the Great Pyramids in Egypt and the Revolutionary and Civil War battlefields in the USA (Timothy 2011, 3). His inventions, which included tourism currency, travel coupons and holiday train tickets, significantly raised public interest in packaged cultural tourism (Franklin 2003, 31).

---

[2] Other early travel agencies include Cox & Kings in 1758 and the Abreu Agency in Porto in 1840.

National Heritage and Tourism

Although early tourism activities were socially contingent to some regions of the world, these forms of heritage tourism were broadly confined to social elites, gentry and nobility (Light 2015). Since the late eighteenth century, however, there has been a public call to appropriate royal family property as 'national heritage'. This is particularly the case in European countries where, after the French Revolution (1789–99), the term *patrimoine* was closely associated with a nationalisation process during which the property of the French monarchy was transformed into a public good (Vecco 2010, 322). The largest public museum in France, the Louvre, was originally a royal museum based on art collections of the monarchy and churches, and now houses thousands of national properties of the arts and sciences. Similarly, the British Museum began with a private collection by the Irish scientist Sir Hans Sloane, and later opened to the public in 1759 as the first national museum of the world.

These national museums reflect colonial and imperialist mentalities derived from explorations of the 'New World'. They also serve as an authoritative source that forms the basis for what Benedict Anderson (1983) called an 'imagined community', and a 'culturally homogeneous and unified' society (Hall 1999, 4). In their seminal work *The Invention of Tradition*, Hobsbawm and Ranger (1983) argued that invented traditions make up the foundation of the modern nation state. To direct and control how the past is interpreted, and to use it for political purposes, governments strategically select sites, practices and events to create a national heritage that mirrors the historical significance of the nation (Wright 2009). In 1851, the Great Exhibition was held in London as the first World Expo showcasing nations' achievements. These exhibitions have played an active role in constructing and interpreting the social memories of nation states and subgroups within national populations.

Following on from Cook's initiatives, heritage tourism grew rapidly during the nineteenth and twentieth centuries. Tourism grew increasingly democratised as travel became cheaper and more accessible. As a consequence of these economic, political and social changes, and an emphasis on national narrative-making efforts, such as those driven by Margaret Thatcher in the UK in the late twentieth century, heritage tourism can represent and serve nationalist policies, spreading this influence outward to international audiences (Timothy and Boyd 2006). Similarly, Cook's mass tourism in the mid-nineteenth century generated an image of a beautiful and peaceful Italy to serve the needs of arrivals (Hom 2015).

As Franklin (2003) has argued, 'the nation-state [became] an important primary agent and constructor of tourism' (25). In the USA and the UK, thanks

Figure 2 Sydney Opera House, Australia

to the mass development of capitalism, a dramatic growth has occurred in heritage tourism, which has led to categorisation, preservation and visitation of heritage sites (Samuel 1994). Respective governments have encouraged the public to visit these heritage sites embedded with national history and natural landscapes. A version of the grand tour was developed in Australia to that end, using sites such as the Sydney Opera House, Great Barrier Reef, the Australian War Memorial and various cultural institutions of each state to commemorate the history of the land and the country.

As a response to or escape from modernity (MacCannell 1976; Hewison 1987), heritage tourism can be regarded as a modern form of alienated consumption driven by a romanticised interest in tradition and authenticity outside of the here and now of everyday life. Accordingly, the public has developed a collective sense of nostalgia through which to engage with the past. Under the UK Thatcher government of the 1980s, policies of national industry restructuring resulted in the mass closure of industrial factories, which led to a boom in the construction of industrial museums (Light 2015, 147). This process of deindustrialisation has been mirrored in other countries such as Germany and Australia, which undertook similar policy changes.

Heritage tourism does not only inform visitors of a glorious national past; it can also include places with difficult or contentious pasts. In South Africa,

Figure 3 Tourists watching the changing of the guard at Buckingham Palace, London, UK

heritage and its associated tourism serves as an essential tool for nation-building after decades of apartheid and social conflict. Furthermore, heritage tourism has become a national education platform to fulfil the social needs of reconciliation and to value the distinctive memories of the black and white populations (Marschall 2009, 1). Similar forms of dark tourism can refer to postcolonial heritages of developing nations (Harrison and Hughes 2010), or the legacy of communism in Central and Eastern Europe (Banaszkiewicz, Graburn and Owsianowska 2017; Light 2000).

In addition to political changes and considerations following war – World War II in particular – several social and economic reasons have spurred the rapid development of heritage tourism. The relatively recent emergence of large-scale tourism has been attributed to, among other factors, a general decrease in working hours, an increase in leisure time and income, and a desire to experience the authentic. Concurrently, tourism is also seen as a powerful tool for nations to use in development strategies. At some heritage sites, local governments have become interest groups with their own entrepreneurial pursuits and policy agendas. For them, heritage tourism is an object of regulation and a means for profit-making.

A good example of such a transformation is the development of the domestic tourism industry in China. During the 1950s, tourism was only a form of special political activity to 'enhance China's political influence and propagate the achievements of socialist reconstruction' – an activity organised for foreign diplomats with permission to visit the country under strict surveillance (Sofield and Li 1998; Sang 2009) and as a reward for 'politically correct' local people such as bureaucrats, schoolteachers and members of the military. Economic reforms in the 1990s transformed the tourism industry from political activity to economic enterprise. Indeed, the building of cross-regional transportation infrastructure in the past decade, such as national highways, high-speed trains and low-cost airlines, was in response to these reforms and resulted in a noticeable increase in domestic travel. In addition, tourism became an essential tool in creating a sense of national unity and domestic economic development, as well as securing foreign exchange (Nakano and Zhu 2020).

World Heritage and Global Tourism

Since World War II, outbound tourism has grown significantly. Mass-scale tourism serves as an effective form of recovering ruined economies and creating new jobs and foreign exchange. The annual number of international tourist arrivals worldwide increased from an average of 25 million in the 1950s to 1.4 billion in 2018, generating approximately US$1.649 trillion globally (UNWTO 2018). Tourism, and its related sectors, is now considered one of the world's largest industries in terms of consumer expenditure and local employment. Much of the growth is attributed to technology, aircraft, highway systems and public transportation. Tourism destinations have largely expanded from limited places in early periods to various isolated countries in the world.

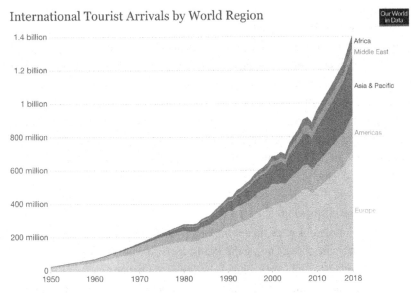

Figure 4 International tourist arrivals by world region

More than forty years have passed since the adoption of the Convention Concerning the Protection of the World Cultural and Natural Heritage by the General Conference of UNESCO in 1972. As of 2020, the World Heritage List included 1,121 properties with contributions from 167 state parties. Similar to the heritage boom in Europe in the nineteenth century as a response to rapid industrialisation, the current global heritage fever reflects a common need for preservation and cultural protection due to rapid social changes driven by capitalism and neoliberalism.

World Heritage inscription has had serious sociocultural and economic impacts on many tourism destinations (Salazar 2010). The 'World Heritage' status UNESCO created has become a globally recognised signifier. While the intention was not to create a tick-a-box list guide for tourists, 'in reality, however, world heritage sites and "wonders" have become just that – "must-see" symbolic attractions in cultural tours, itineraries, tour operator and tourist board marketing' (Evans 2004, 316, cited in Salazar and Zhu 2015). This is largely because the term 'world' highlights universal value and significance. Consequently, World Heritage designation 'is increasingly becoming an integral part of site or destination marketing campaigns' (Leask and Fyall 2006, 287). For international tourists, UNESCO's list of World Heritage Sites is

Figure 5 World Heritage emblem of the historical centre of Riga

regarded as official. Such recognition has created a sense of trust that tourists can easily follow the list without questioning the significance of the sites.

Tourism was not considered within the UNESCO World Heritage Convention (WHC) in the early days, however. The original 1977 Operational Guidelines for the Implementation of the World Heritage Convention document does not engage with tourism as one of its main themes. Subsequent versions of the guidelines have treated tourism as a potential threat to heritage, linked to poor heritage management (Salazar and Zhu 2015, 246). The discourse of 'threat' has dominated related heritage policies for many years. Such concerns mainly refer to developing countries that heavily rely on tourism for economic growth, and that are particularly susceptible to natural and social changes. This discourse emphasises the negative impacts of tourism.

UNESCO has gradually recognised the value of the tourism industry for preserving cultural heritage. In the 2019 version of the Operational Guidelines, tourism was acknowledged as 'one factor of [the] economy' (UNESCO 2019). It also suggested the idea of 'visitor management, which needs to gather information on tourism activities' (UNESCO 2019). This is reflected in other heritage policies and guidelines such as the 2003 Convention for the Safeguarding of Intangible Cultural Heritage.

Figure 6 Western tourists at Durbar Square in Bhaktapur, Nepal

The recognition of tourism in heritage was quickly considered by UNESCO's advisory bodies and other non-governmental organisations (NGOs). These organisations built strategies and policies to consider heritage and tourism together while treating tourism as a 'tool for development' (Bourdeau, Gravari-Barbas and Robinson 2015, 16). The International Council on Monuments and Sites (ICOMOS) launched the Charter of Cultural Tourism in 1976 to promote heritage conservation while considering the impacts of tourism development on local communities.

Similarly, the United Nations World Tourism Organization (UNWTO) and the United Nations Environment Programme (UNEP) have developed the concept of sustainable tourism and related principles and guidelines that refer to the environmental, economic and sociocultural aspects of tourism development. According to the UNWTO, sustainable tourism is defined as practices that:[3]

- Make optimal use of environmental resources that constitute a crucial element in tourism development, maintaining essential ecological processes and helping to conserve natural heritage and biodiversity.
- Respect the sociocultural authenticity of host communities, conserve their built and living cultural heritage and traditional values, and contribute to intercultural understanding and tolerance.
- Ensure viable, long-term economic operations, providing socio-economic benefits to all stakeholders that are fairly distributed, including stable employment and income-earning opportunities and social services to host communities, and contributing to poverty alleviation.

Drawing on the initiatives of sustainable tourism, international organisations recognise the severe damage mass tourism may cause to countries and their natural environment. Certain guidelines and initiatives, such as the World Heritage Alliance for Sustainable Tourism (2006–10) and the Friends of World Heritage, were created to raise awareness and promote sustainable tourism (Salazar and Zhu 2015, 246).

Although different countries around the world have accepted sustainable tourism, the concept has been criticised as an externally imposed Western paradigm of modernisation without the capacity to address the inequalities and needs of communities (Jamal 2019, 147). The actual impacts of these policies on the ground are questionable. Sustainable tourism and other similar concepts may be used as a mechanism to legitimise certain stakeholders' economic, social or political agendas. Subsequently, the interaction between different stakeholders on international, national or local scales often leads to

---

[3] www.unwto.org/sustainable-development

conflicting interests within the tourism field, which stimulates intellectual speculation concerning the politics of heritage tourism.

3 Politics of Heritage Tourism

This section reviews the impact of global forces in the tourism industry on heritage sites and their associated communities. Power is a central issue here, showing the capacity of ideas and ideologies in influencing people's lives. Heritage and tourism are not merely a modern form of cultural production and consumption; they are regarded as political, social and cultural phenomena situated in a global context.

This section is titled 'Politics of Heritage Tourism' as I unravel the previous and still existing social and cultural relations of power in heritage tourism and their consequences. Here the exercise of power is not only about authority, the state and political and institutional systems. Power also incorporates 'micro' governmental practices to reveal the connection between the 'political' and other power relations, practices and technologies (Foucault 1982; Coles and Church 2007, 25).

I explore in detail how power has been constructed within the heritage tourism industry, focusing on several 'grand narratives' and ideologies that have dominated meaning-making practices for centuries. Overarching ideologies such as imperialism and nationalism have had a significant influence on how cultural heritage has been understood, empowering expert-approved sites, buildings and artefacts that ultimately become the locus of heritage tourism. These ideas, often driven by Western countries, provide a global system of values and beliefs, leading heritage tourism to direct cultural policies and economic activities in other countries (especially developing countries). Simultaneously, governments of affected countries use heritage tourism as a political tool for nation-building and economic development. Such value appropriation might lead to social stratification resulting from unquestioning expert governance, class or race (Zhu and Maags 2020).

Here, I do not intend to deny many best practices of heritage tourism on the ground; they offer creativity and positive social, economic and cultural impacts on local societies. Before visiting these issues in the next two sections, I concentrate in this section on heritage tourism within the debates of global cultural hegemony. Heritage and tourism facilitate the establishment of social relations and practices that legitimise the ways we understand the world and our past. In so doing, heritage tourism is not an independent entity, but a political and social field in which powerful actors engage in multiple and complex interactions across time and space. This engagement consequently transforms the discourse of heritage tourism from cultural and economic topics into political debates. These debates often consider inequality, landownership, changes to people's livelihood and social and cultural differences.

Imperialism: Transnational Organisations and the Tourist Gaze

In the past decades, especially after the Cold War, many scholars have criticised the cultural, economic and political impact of Western power on the rest of the world. Edward Said, in his 1993 collection of essays, traced the connection between imperialism and culture since the eighteenth century. Said (1993, 8) defined imperialism as 'the practice, the theory, and the attitudes of a dominating metropolitan centre ruling a distant territory'. While this tangible and geographically bound definition has mostly eroded since the end of World War II (following the independence of several colonised nations), its legacy continues through cultural and economic influences, especially in globalisation processes (Tomlinson 1991). To understand the roots of this legacy and its continued impact, it is necessary, according to Said (1978, 1993), to understand how colonialist and imperialist nations used 'culture' to influence and control other nations.

The critical question is whether heritage tourism is part of the global practice of economic and cultural imperialism. If so, how does heritage tourism facilitate the formation of power that shapes the asymmetrical relationship between developed and developing countries? I believe these questions are embedded in the history of heritage tourism as an international process of value creation and negotiation.

In Section 2, I examined the global history of heritage tourism that has been grounded in social changes occurring in Western societies. Both the grand tour in the seventeenth and eighteenth centuries and the early form of heritage tourism during the nineteenth century have been associated with the Enlightenment spirit and the growing concern for preserving the natural and cultural environment within the public consciousness (Harrison 2013). In the late twentieth century, along with the rise of modern consumption, globalisation became the primary cause for cultural imperialism. Embedded within Western discourses, the emergence of international institutions, policies and technologies has meant a predominance of Western-oriented ideas that drive heritage tourism (Winter 2009). This value system has formed the backbone of the heritage tourism industry in all countries, whether they are part of the Global South or North. These ideas and cultural norms have spread across the globe and have turned tourism into a form of Western imperialism (Nash 1989).

As part of this global imperialism, heritage tourism has a significant impact on the world's economy, politics and culture. Three powerful key actors use political and economic instruments to spread global cultural values and habits to influence other parts of the world. First, international organisations such as the UNWTO and UNESCO play critical roles in establishing cultural policies and ethical codes to create global standards concerning what is considered good, beautiful and appropriate (Smith 2006). These heritage tourism policies have (re)defined the meaning of culture by applying particular types of language and ethical principles. These global values and standards, historically disseminated by European colonial powers, view local heritage through the lens of political dominance and assumed cultural superiority (Herzfeld 2004).[4]

For local communities, the global standards and values created by international organisations compete with their interests (Herzfeld 2006). When transnational organisations dominate the local tourism industry, cultural practices often get overshadowed by a language of universal morality to maintain the international standard. As such, heritage site management often integrates professional knowledge and policies without considering local communities' voices.

Second, international tourism companies shape the imaginaries of 'the host nation's value systems, beliefs, lifestyles and consumption patterns (Sinclair-Maragh and Gursoy 2015, 148). In this context, tourism has become an instrument of economic power, particularly in postcolonial nations in the Pacific, Asia, Africa and South America. At the same time, transnational enterprises such as Lonely Planet and Tripadvisor intentionally accommodate Western tourist interests by promoting and rebuilding the images of local customs, arts and crafts (Craik 1994). In some postcolonial areas, Western residents have developed the tourism industry for Western visitors, while indigenous people only serve as workers and performers.

Third, tourist expectations shape the relationship between tourists and hosts. Drawing on Foucault's concept of the 'medical gaze', Urry (1990) analysed tourism as an organised and regulated social practice. According to Urry (1990), the 'tourist gaze' is situated in an imagined world which emphasises exoticness or otherness to create the tourist experience. A tourist's viewpoint has been manipulated 'so that the gaze falls upon what the gazer expects to see' (Turner, Turner and Carroll 2005, 293).

In a study of Maasai tourism in Kenya, Bruner and Kirshenblatt-Gimblett (1994) found that Maasai performers would act in such a way as to

---

[4] In recent decades, non-Western states from Asia, Africa and Latin America have sent people to work in these international organisations, showing their attempts to increase their voice in global policymaking.

Figure 7 Cultural performance in Hawaii, USA

accommodate the expectations of their white patrons. Their re-enactment of colonial British-Maasai encounters is a way of earning money rather than maintaining their traditional history. The Maasai case demonstrates how tourism (particularly postcolonial tourism) can create a colonial gaze to shape the relationship between local communities and public audiences (Eeden 2004). The guest symbolises a bourgeois identity within this context, while the host represents an exotic tourism spectacle. The power imbalance between host and guest is reinforced into a public display through heritage tourism.

Through powerful agents such as international organisations, tourism enterprises and tourists (and their gaze), heritage tourism has become a resource for cultural and economic imperialism. Unlike military dominance in the past, this hegemonic cultural and economic influence is not created through physical control, but through ideology and value systems (Gramsci 1971). This type of social control is more hidden than previous colonisation, as it is created within societies as a consistent process of image building. As such, heritage tourism contributes to the oppression, domination, misrecognition and stereotyping of host communities (Jamal 2019, 90).

Capitalism, Commodification and Authenticity

Along with cultural imperialism, it is essential to frame international tourism as a continuing feature of capitalism, considering the worldwide export of capitalist practices following World War II. In this way, tourism is seen as cultural production and an economic and industrial venture (d'Hauteserre 2006). It provides a wide-ranging and valuable resource for economic and social development on all scales of governance. Investment in tourism therefore becomes a national resource requiring the employment of people, creation of supportive infrastructure and investment of capital.

Heritage tourism is part of this discussion. As Hewison (1989, 22) indicated, the heritage tourism industry has become dictated by consumer demand and ulterior motives instead of the values promoted by the UNESCO Heritage Convention (including stewardship and sustainability). Many alleged consequences of heritage tourism are the features of capitalism in general. In what follows, I focus on two issues: exploitation and displacement as a consequence of the tourism industry, and plural meanings of authenticity as derived from the commodification of heritage tourism.

Exploitation and Displacement

Tourism, as Britton (1991, 451) remarked, is an essential vehicle of capitalist accumulation. From the Marxist and neo-Marxist perspectives, the dynamics of international tourism development continue to be driven by the imperatives of profit-making and the exploitation of wage labour (Perrons 1999, 94). Aligned with neoliberal globalisation, international tourism encourages the growth of large transnational tourism enterprises. They often become the key sectors dominating the markets and distribution channels (Mosedale 2006).

Like other transnational industries, the dominance of international enterprises in tourism, especially in developing countries, often leads to the exploitation of indigenous communities as low-level labourers. In East Africa, South Pacific islands and the Caribbean, a conspicuous lack of indigenous involvement exists in financing and managing tourism (Harrison 1992, 23; 2001, 31).

Even worse, the development of the tourism industry at heritage sites can sometimes legitimise the redistribution of land and resources, resulting in the symbolic displacement and gentrification of certain areas (Bammer 1994). This is the case of tourism development in the town of Dali, China, which led to a 'symbolic displacement' of local ethnic people in order to facilitate the construction of antique-like architecture, theme parks and ethnic touristic performances (Notar 2006). Similarly, the development of large resorts in Huatulco, Mexico resulted in the eviction of farmers who were subsequently forced to abandon their independent, family-owned businesses to seek work in the largest foreign-dominated industry (Camacho 1996). In both cases, indigenous culture can become 'museumified', and local communities grow marginalised and alienated.

Figure 8 Souvenir shops in Paris, France

The reality is complex in terms of the dynamics between local and transnational tourism enterprises. Tourism can often lead to jobs and other economic opportunities. In Borobudur, Indonesia, tourism provides locals employment as souvenir vendors, guides and guest house owners (Nuryanti 1996).

However, in many parts of the world, much of the benefit derived from the tourism industry is invested with foreign groups and international tourism companies who take a large share of the profits gained by local communities (Salazar and Zhu 2015). Only a minimal amount of tourism profit (one fifth to one third) stays in local communities (Ashley 2006). Rather than contributing to equality and social welfare, heritage tourism can facilitate the 'accumulation of dispossession' due to capitalistic dominance (Harvey 2004). The issue here is not the degree to which the local communities (of heritage sites) have become involved in the tourism business. Instead, the key issue is the power relations embedded in decision-making and management. It is more significant to identify who has the power to define heritage and design tourism products, and who reaps the benefit of the industry.

Authenticity and Commodification

In addition to labour exploitation and displacement, another issue of capitalistic tourism is commodification, or, more precisely, the action of turning culture into a commodity (Appadurai 1988). The notion of authenticity appears as a central point of scholarly discussion on the relationship between heritage tourism and commodification (e.g. Wang 1999).

Authenticity is a contestable idea, yet the term is primarily used (within heritage tourism) to describe certain tourists' motivations (Salazar and Zhu 2015). In this context, the search for 'authenticity' underpins tourist behaviour and interest in travel. The forms of 'authentic' heritage are varied, but can include traditional ethnic or indigenous culture (both tangible and intangible) and preserved landscapes (Zhu 2012). While scholars may contend that the authentic means the actual reality of something, tourists may not wish to see this reality and instead seek a staged 'authentic' experience (MacCannell 1976). They often bring their agendas, imaginaries of a place or previous experience of the site when they encounter heritage (McIntosh and Prentice 1999).

As a consequence of 'authenticity seeking', tourism operators and service providers have responded in kind, staging an 'authentic' experience to match tourists' expectations and desires (MacCannell 1976). Heritage sites become consumable products to enhance the tourist experience (Salazar and Zhu 2015). Cultural festivals, traditionally exclusive for local communities, often become commercialised for touristic purposes and disseminated to outsiders (Richards

Figure 9 Roman soldier walking tour, Rome, Italy

2007). Many scholars, including Boorstin (1964), criticise such transformations as 'pseudo-events' that result in a loss of meaning.

This is the case in the well-documented Alarde celebration in Basque towns of Spain. Alarde was originally a community celebration of a historic victory in battle over the troops of King Louis XIII of France in the siege of AD 1638. This celebration is a re-enactment of local solidarity and historical identity where all members of the local community (poor and rich) stood together against oppressors. Once the Spanish municipal government designed the celebration to be held twice in the same day to attract more external visitors, the local Basques became less interested in celebrating the festival. Such tourism promotion changed the original purpose of the event (Greenwood 1989).

Conversely, Cohen (1988) argues that heritage value is not necessarily destroyed by commodification. Instead, tourism-created or altered products can become imbued with new meanings and cultural nuances adopted by local communities, becoming a part of their cultural identity. Even Greenwood (1989, 181) changed his mind and later indicated that the commodified Alarde celebration can 'become a much more public event and is imbued now with contemporary political significance as part of the contestation over regional political rights in Spain'. Accordingly, commodification does not necessarily always degrade the local culture, but can instead give new life to the community.

So what are the actual effects of commodification on cultural heritage in the tourism industry? Does such a process lead to value erosion of local culture, or does it offer new meanings? This is a complicated question as meanings and value are culturally and spatially based, and the academic debate about authenticity continues. Within this context, authenticity is understood as a socially constructed idea, dependant on emotion, feelings of belonging and connection, rather than an objective lens through which to view things (Wang 1999; Cohen and Cohen 2012). However, expert-led heritage tourism often neglects both tourists and cultural practitioners' emotions in their decision-making practices. This lack of recognition within the authenticity debate stems from a power imbalance between hosts, brokers and guests (Porter and Salazar 2005).

Above all, two primary consequences of capitalism can be seen to affect heritage tourism. These discussions addressed the uneven nature of tourism and capitalist development and the systematic variations in the local conditions of tourism development (Mosedale 2010). The distribution of wealth created by a power imbalance between the tourists, tourism operators and local communities has dictated the establishment of the heritage tourism market (Britton 1982). Within this industry, wealthy tourists augment how heritage tourism is considered, presented and encountered, which leads to the exacerbation of existing class and racial divides (Gmelch 2003). Ultimately, this tension is reinforced by governments seeking to use tourism as a profit-oriented industry while carefully controlling and constructing heritage to satisfy tourist expectations.

Nationalism: Amnesia, Cultural Objectification and Spatial Cleansing

As shown in the previous sections, national identity relies on establishing certain heritage narratives to reinforce the symbolic foundation of nations. Nation states are based on a 'shared common past, culture, language, and history among mobile workers engendered by the technologies of travel in the context of industrialisation' (Gellner 1983; Mookherjee 2011, 4). Formerly achieved through kinship or race, nation-building is now realised by governmental use of political power (Anderson 1983). In expressing this power, certain cultural heritages (monuments, festivals and performances) are used to generate a cohesive national connection and homogeneity – creating a unified imaginary of the nation's beginnings (Palmer 1998). These heritage products portray an official discourse that directs tourists' engagement with and understanding of that nation's history (Pretes 2003).

As Timothy and Boyd (2006, 3) point out, heritage is sometimes a powerful tool to spread propaganda to international visitors and patriotic education at the domestic level. This is particularly true in socialist and communist regimes where heritage attractions often support certain political ideologies (Henderson 2007). The itinerary for a trip to North Korea is carefully designed to include critical strategic places such as war museums, monuments and government buildings. On the border between North and South Korea, propaganda villages and the demilitarised zone (DMZ) have been established in the name of unification to show a staged living environment of life from both sides (Henderson 2002). Another example is the recent development of red tourism in China that exploits the historical heritage of the Chinese Communist Party to sustain the Communist identity (Li, Hu and Zhang 2010). Similar forms of heritage tourism have also emerged in post-communist countries such as Hungary and Romania (Light 2000).

Patriotic education does not only aim at domestic tourists but also concerns diaspora communities residing outside their ancestral lands. Here, the cultural heritage of the host country plays a significant role in producing certain perceptions of the homeland that connect the diaspora and the host as one 'imagined community' (Anderson 1983; Zhu 2020). In Scotland, annual homecoming festivals have attracted millions of tourists to experience an imagined but 'authentic' Scottish cultural heritage (Bryce, Murdy and Alexander 2017).

Figure 10 The reunification statue at the third tunnel of the DMZ, South Korea

Figure 11 Red tourism in Yan'an, China

However, heritage tourism does not merely involve peaceful processes of using cultural practices for nationalist purposes. To establish and legitimise national political regimes, cultural narratives for heritage tourism often use specific cultural techniques and strategies to fulfil national political purposes. Three common practices achieve these political purposes: (1) remembering and forgetting certain histories to foster social cohesion; (2) regulating lower-class and minority groups through cultural objectification; and (3) highlighting national narratives by separating heritage space from daily life.

First, while designing heritage tourism content, nation states include and exclude particular kinds of histories for commemoration and public display. The selection and use of heritage sites, memorials and museums therefore involve a cultural amnesia. As part of this process, certain past narratives are erased while others are constructed to generate evidence of shared heritage or nationhood.

Narratives particularly susceptible to this cultural amnesia are varied, though most concern particularly dark periods in a state's history. These narratives tend to dwell on revolutions, colonialism, wars, civil unrest, massacres and ethnic exclusions that still have resounding impacts on many citizens who remember the events (Logan and Reeves 2009). These negative historical issues often challenge the building of national and social cohesion. Once these historical events are transformed into narratives for heritage tourism, some aspects of the past are forgotten or repressed for political uses. In other words, heritage tourism facilitates the state's practices of cultural amnesia and memory distortion, turning unsettled pasts into instrumental resources for nation-building. As Shumway (1991) argues, these 'guiding fictions' shape people's understanding and connection to the nation – their national identity (xi).

In many Caribbean countries, heritage tourism often focuses on the sun, sea and sand without recognising the colonial influence on local societies or their lived experiences of this history (Cameron and Gatewood 2011). Similarly, the dark history of slavery was often left out of heritage tourism development in the USA and the UK. Although both countries have recently started to recognise these difficult pasts, the cultural representation of the narratives still involves negotiation and contestation between stakeholders of differing political ideologies and agendas (Seaton 2001).

Second, nation states often use heritage tourism to establish 'an ethnocentric hierarchy' that conforms to the culture and tradition of the state (Zhu, Jin and Graburn 2017). Defined as 'cultural objectification' (Handler 1988), this process is regarded as a fundamental national strategy in establishing a connected or ongoing relationship between state-endorsed sociocultural traditions and their ethnic people, who become objectified as a marker of authenticity

(Wood 1997). This issue is particularly evident in Asia and the Pacific, where central and local governments often function as 'planners of tourist development, as the marketer of cultural meanings, and as the arbiter of cultural practices displayed to tourists' (Wood 1984, 353). As a result, local and regional indigenous cultures may sometimes be claimed as 'icons' of national heritage, especially in settler-colonial nations, such as Maori in New Zealand, Inca in Peru, Eskimos in Alaska and Inuit in Canada.

Heritage tourism often conforms to Western conceptions of ethnicity, transforming fluid, nested and changeable identities into something 'mutually exclusive' and exotic (Wood 1984). Similar to other countries in Asia, Chinese governments define, regulate and develop the ethnic tourism industry to facilitate the cultivation of ethnic identity while integrating ethnic groups into the state economy (Graburn 2015; Zhu 2018a). As a result, Han Chinese are presented as modern and civilised, while ethnic people are portrayed as backward, feminine and exotic (Schein 1997). This classification legitimises the state ideology of Marxism and its 'stages of history' approach in which ethnic groups are often portrayed as 'living fossils' (Oakes 1993, 54).

Third, nationalism is often celebrated through national landmarks such as monuments and archaeological sites and their associated official histories while de-emphasising ordinary people's lives. Subsequently, the planning and management of heritage tourism often involve separating the space of heritage from people's daily lives by creating zoning laws, safety standards and physical boundaries of walls and fences (Zhu 2015). Such processes, phrased as 'spatial cleansing' by Michael Herzfeld (2006), aim to create a large open space that implies 'permanence, eternity, [and] the disappearance of temporality' of the national past that leads to social stratification and displacement (129).

These issues are particularly observable in places where heritage discourse is used to control people's engagement with their local environment. The city of Xi'an, China is undergoing a redevelopment process in which its cultural heritage mirrors discourses of beauty and national pride as the main focus of heritage tourism development. The city's physical environment was recreated in an image that would appeal to tourists, investors and modern aesthetics of the national past. The monumentalism of heritage buildings, wide boulevards and imperial public spaces creates a sense of space that echoes national narratives of permanence and authenticity. The local Muslim residential area was turned into a Muslim food street and became one of the popular heritage tourism destinations.

In his study of heritage developments in Greek, Italian and Thai cities, Herzfeld (2006) demonstrated this process to be an active policy that regulated people's views of heritage. A similar phenomenon took place in India: the local governments, aligned with archaeologists, embraced a nationalist ideology of

Figure 12 City wall in Xi'an, China

the material past, leading to the 'spatial cleansing' of the village of Hampi (Bloch 2016). In this process, heritage sites and objects were collected, isolated, decontextualised and displayed for tourists' consumption to glorify the nation state, whilst residents faced eviction or restricted livelihoods in associated areas. These actions often involve physical destruction, urban gentrification and sometimes dispossession (Meskell 2019).

Above all, heritage tourism not only facilitates the representation and reinforcement of cultural or national identity; it also generates conflicting social and political impacts on local communities. The issues mentioned here (amnesia, cultural objectification and spatial cleansing) are only some of the many cultural effects heritage tourism has created in different countries around the world. These effects not only show the political nature of heritage, but also illustrate how powerful agents such as nation states can utilise heritage tourism in spatial and cultural governance. As seen from the preceding examples, the production of heritage tourism for nationalist agendas might create various social and political impacts on local communities, especially those who do not share the same understanding of the official narratives of their heritage within or apart from national history.

However, it is not always the case that national control over heritage tourism development creates tensions and conflicts. Local communities can sometimes develop a good relationship with the state through the promotion of their cultural heritage. One such relationship is demonstrated in Canadian Inuit art that emerged in the late 1940s as Inuits sought to retain their indigenous heritage, which was under threat due to lifestyle changes brought upon by modernisation. Such cultural production matched Canada's interest in developing their distinctive national heritage in contrast to the USA. Subsequently, the state governments have been supportive of the promotion of Inuit art: one of the key components of Canadian cultural heritage that local Inuit communities are proud of (Graburn 2004). These collaborations between local communities and states lead to the creative work of heritage tourism discussed in the section titled 'Co-production'.

Cultural Elitism: Knowledge Production and Social Exclusion

Each of the issues discussed so far has been orchestrated via a level of knowledge production bound to experts, elites and nation states. The language created by heritage organisations and professionals is used to (re)construct the past in specific ways so as to consolidate elite interests (Nora 1989; Smith 2006). Within governing charters, policies and related articles such as those produced by UNESCO, these languages dictate how people understand their past (Smith 2006, 4).

This expert-driven influence in understanding heritage, let alone how the past is interacted with, leads to two critical questions about agency: who controls heritage, and how it is constructed. Heritage tourism – its production and management – is situated within the domain of certain organised (national and international) institutions and professionals. Through international conventions and laws, ideas about heritage conservation and tourism development have become internationally naturalised to the extent that the principles presented have become 'common sense' (Smith 2006).

Here, I do not intend to suggest that the professionalisation of heritage tourism is morally wrong. Quite the opposite – professionals are necessary as experts in undertaking heritage assessments and management that constitute 'highly specialised operations' and complex threshold criteria (Harrison 2010, 35). Heritage and tourism professionals use these international standards, policies and charters to access, record, interpret and manage heritage tourism sites. These standards often integrate specific ethics codes to regulate how professionals and experts should practise in their respective countries. Experts need to ensure that certain standards are met in governing quality and assurance of heritage (Colley 2015, 15).

However, these experts and professionals employed to manage heritage-related sites and tourism activities are all too often procured or defined by middle-class ideologies (Waterton and Smith 2010). The heritage purported by these groups often reflects elite social practices and experiences or 'high culture' that are not representative of reality, or at least do not encompass all aspects of culture (Herzfeld 2015). Furthermore, these experts often emphasise aesthetics of culture such as beauty, order, magnificence and harmony (particularly in Asian contexts) to serve the purpose of 'social distinction' (Bourdieu 1984). Consequently, the general public, especially the poor, the less educated, ethnic minorities, and other marginal groups, is often excluded from management and heritage interpretation.

Power imbalances are inevitable when professionals, experts and elites dominate the design and planning of heritage tourism and other relevant industries. The power structure of cultural elitism and knowledge production is implemented through two stages: institutionalisation and recognition.

First, heritage tourism development often results in the establishment of new political institutions. Today, heritage tourism sites are often directly regulated by state administrative organisations such as heritage, tourism and planning departments. Supported by these institutions, the state takes over the role as custodian of both the national and the local pasts. After creating a formal legal and organisational framework, authorities and experts are empowered to select the official representative of the regional or national heritage tourism destinations. In other words, non-state actors such as architects, archaeologists and tourism planners become experts in planning and decision-making. Consequently, the autonomy of communities and traditional cultural practitioners previously involved in the use and preservation of sites and cultural practices has been weakened.

Second, the establishment of heritage tourism destinations often involves a process of recognition – a procedure in which heritage sites are recognised through official evaluation and selection for tourism development. Once something has been recognised as 'authentic' heritage, it is often regarded as being of aesthetic, cultural and, at times, sacred value. Conversely, cultural sites and practices that have not been selected as heritage are considered inauthentic and may be disrespected, devalued or ignored (Zhu 2015).

Furthermore, such systems of recognition tend to provide an idealised version of heritage tourism that heavily relies on professional, institutionalised knowledge and expertise to fulfil upper-class or middle-class demands while ignoring local communities' needs. In this sense, non-elite groups of local communities can only contribute minimally, if at all, in the tourism planning and governance process (Moscardo 2011, 424). In Senegal, the identification of the Kankurang masked performance as an intangible cultural heritage (ICH) changed the history and meaning of the performance. Whereas it once inspired rebellion, it has been altered to reflect the restoration of order – a rite in which participants are taught social standards of respect, solidarity, courage and humility (De Jong 2016, 173).

Nowadays, the criticism of this power imbalance within the heritage industry also concerns the relationship between the expert and community (Waterton and Smith 2010). Key to this discussion is who owns and has access to heritage (Harrison 2013, 109). In John Schofield's (2016) edited collection *Who Needs Experts?* scholars have noticed a recent democratic movement concerning the ownership of heritage and public participation in recognising and celebrating community-based cultural heritage (Lowenthal 2015). Indeed, both the Burra Charter (Australia, 1979) and the Faro Convention (Europe, 2005) emphasise the need to engage with the public, not just experts, to ensure the inclusion of all cultural participants. Such a democratised approach within heritage tourism is discussed further in the next sections.

Summary and Discussion

This section explores several political issues hidden behind the cultural, social and economic benefits of heritage tourism. It shows how Western ideological value systems have become globalised and influential in non-Western countries. International organisations, tourism enterprises and professionals all play significant roles in facilitating the expansion of cultural imperialism and capitalism.

This section does not intend to create a simple dichotomy between Western and non-Western value systems, or between developed and developing countries. Instead, this section exposes the uneven power structures behind the beautiful and profitable mask of heritage tourism. Some international organisations and enterprises shape and control these power structures. More importantly, the ideas and ideologies created by these institutions have been incorporated into nation states to legitimise their pursuit of political, economic and sociocultural agendas. As a result, heritage tourism has become a tool for imperialism, nation-building, economic development and social stratification.

Subsequently, heritage tourism is closely associated with neoliberal governance and the dominance of capitalism. Driven by local states, urban elites and tourism enterprises, the development of heritage tourism might result in a dramatic transformation of heritage sites that leads to gentrification, displacement and the loss of traditional artisanship (Harvey 2008; Herzfeld 2015). Consequently, poor heritage tourism management might create various forms of domination and injustice such as cultural degradation, exclusion, manipulation and oppression (Young 1990).

Furthermore, as heritage tourism is often associated with 'good' and valuable effects such as 'beauty', 'pride' or 'profit', it is easier for the governing bodies (and those professionals associated with them) to create societal consensus in decision-making during the process of heritage tourism production and management. Compared to other development projects such as real estate or the mining industry, the dominance over heritage tourism might be confronted with less opposition from the public – the need for non-expert community involvement is downplayed. Heritage tourism becomes a soft but useful resource in depoliticising the space controlled by powerful agents while their social, economic and political interests are reinforced.

Discovering the politics of heritage tourism and their influences on societies is only the first step of this research. Several complex questions remain regarding the hope and possibilities for emancipation. How can we conduct 'morally good' actions in heritage tourism? Whose rights and which rights should be considered in decision-making and planning? Is there a way to acknowledge communities' voices in the process of recognition, interpretation and management? Can heritage tourism move away from exploitation and dispossession and contribute to cultural equity and social justice? All of these questions are discussed in the next sections.

4 Empowerment and Challenges

In the previous section, I addressed how power is expressed, articulated and used by international organisations, national institutions and individuals in the heritage tourism industry. The asymmetries of power might lead to misrecognition and misrepresentation of cultural values and to the exclusion of certain marginalised groups. In the past decades, international organisations and NGOs have recognised the challenges of top-down approaches to tourism development and its negative impacts on heritage sites and their communities. The producers of heritage have begun to take note of the voices of minority, ethnic and marginal peoples against a backdrop of global democracy and environmental movements (Lowenthal 2015). Accordingly, international organisations have advocated and designed alternative instruments to recognise communities' livelihoods while serving the needs of heritage tourism, especially in developing countries.

In the 1990s, international recognition of the need to address issues of cultural value and diversity, particularly within UNESCO, started gaining momentum. The promotion of cultural diversity has led to the emergence of various heritage-related concepts, which now include intangible heritage and the cultural landscape (Aikawa-Faure 2009, 15–17). These concepts are used to grasp the plural forms of cultural heritage worldwide and to add value to the sociocultural environment in which tourism practices are embedded. These alternate approaches often challenge European traditions of heritage conservation (Nagaoka 2015).

This section illustrates the ways international organisations use certain concepts and practices, such as cultural landscapes, intangible heritage and eco-museums, in heritage tourism for cultural recognition and resource redistribution. In doing so, heritage tourism can be used to help local communities exert control over social, economic and political factors that affect their lives.

This transfer of power from external institutions to local communities has become known as 'empowerment', a popular term among NGOs and international organisations within policy development. (Laverack and Wallerstein 2001). According to Timothy (2007), empowerment is both a capacity and a process that shifts decision-making and resource distribution from authorities, external experts and investors to community members. These instruments allow local individuals and communities to build cultural awareness and identity while promoting their social and economic interests.

However, the good intentions of 'empowerment' might not always lead to the expected results on the ground. The implementation of these instruments around the world has often been confronted by challenges generated from policy transfer, existing power structures within nation states and internal community politics. The alternative ways of recognising cultural values for developing heritage tourism might even legitimise the capital exploitation and maldistribution of cultural resources.

Intangible Heritage and Tourism

Soon after adopting the UNESCO WHC in 1972, representatives of predominant countries from the Global South criticised the Eurocentric notion of cultural heritage and its heavy focus on material, tangible forms of culture (Hafstein 2009; Steiner and Frey 2012). During the 1980s, UNESCO made numerous attempts to address these concerns, such as cooperating with the World Intellectual Property Organization (WIPO) to develop model provisions for the protection of folklore and adopting the Recommendation on the Safeguarding of Traditional Culture and Folklore in 1989 (Aikawa 2004, 137–8).

East Asian countries have been very influential in promoting 'intangible' cultural practices as a response to the criticism of the focus on material culture (Aikawa 2004). Japan, having joined UNESCO in 1991, started to promote its notion of 'intangible heritage' based on the Japanese Living National Treasure system developed during the American occupation in the 1950s in order to safeguard Japanese traditions after World War II. This system encouraged cultural practitioners to transmit their cultural knowledge and skills to the next generation by providing them with an official title and stipend. Although UNESCO had already been undergoing a shift towards recognising the value of folklore, East Asian countries' efforts were decisive in conceptualising their culture as 'immaterial' or 'intangible' forms of heritage – thus elevating folklore to the status of 'heritage'.

In addition to the call from East Asian countries, the push to develop a new approach within UNESCO for the safeguarding of immaterial heritage was initiated by the Spanish poet and novelist Juan Goytisolo. In 1996, Goytisolo wrote a letter to request the official recognition of Jemaa'el-Fna Square in Marrakech, Morocco as a 'cultural space' so the market could be saved from destruction as a result of modern urbanisation initiatives (Aikawa-Faure 2009, 16). He suggested that the square had artistic and historical values that resembled the 'oral heritage of humanity' (Schmitt 2008, 100). Following that initiative, in Marrakech, in June 1997, UNESCO issued the Proclamation of Masterpieces of the Oral and Intangible Heritage of Humanity and three masterpieces lists (2001, 2003 and 2005). However, the Masterpieces Proclamation has been criticised as promoting an elitist notion of culture (Hafstein 2009, 98).

Since then, UNESCO has organised several meetings to develop a new instrument and Convention. After a long-term process of refining the definition and scope of ICH, the paradigm shift to include intangible heritage was finally completed when UNESCO adopted the Convention for the Safeguarding of Intangible Cultural Heritage in 2003 (UNESCO 2003). The Convention defined intangible cultural heritage as:

> the practices, representations, expressions, knowledge, skills – as well as the instruments, objects, artefacts and cultural spaces associated therewith – that communities, groups and, in some cases, individuals recognise as part of their cultural heritage. This intangible cultural heritage, transmitted from generation to generation, is constantly recreated by communities and groups in response to their environment, their interaction with nature and their history, and provides them with a sense of identity and continuity, thus promoting respect for cultural diversity and human creativity. (UNESCO 2003)

In contrast to the previous paradigm embedded in the WHC, the Convention emphasises the need for a community-based, participatory approach to safeguarding ICH (Kurin 2004, 68). The Convention's Representative List is meant to demonstrate 'representative' examples of community culture and cultural diversity, rather than the previous notions of 'Outstanding Universal Value' and 'authenticity' (Hafstein 2009, 100–2; Skounti 2009, 77–8). In addition, traditional bearers of cultural practices have been the focus in the definition and policymaking of intangible heritage.

In consideration of the importance of ICH in policymaking, in 2012 the UNWTO recognised the links between tourism and ICH, identifying the challenges, risks and opportunities for tourism development related to ICH (Salazar and Zhu 2015). Through a compilation of case studies, the report considered steps to identify, manage and promote ICH as part of government, public/private partnerships and community initiatives. These steps were identified in recognition of the UNWTO's assessment of tourism as a mechanism to provide employment, alleviate poverty, incentivise less rural migration and generate pride within community groups. However, the report also recognised the instability of ICH, noting how miscommunication and misrecognition between various parties can create divisions. Nonetheless, the UNWTO's recognition of ICH in heritage tourism has been an essential step in facilitating change in heritage recognition and community capacity building.

The recognition of ICH as a new category in the tourism context represents a shift from a materialistic approach to a humanistic approach. It is supposed to empower once marginalised groups (including local practitioners and communities) by endowing them with the ability to value and interpret their own heritage (Esfehani and Albrecht 2018). UNESCO's recognition of the Caribbean region as fiscally and culturally underrepresented on the World Heritage List led to the Caribbean Community and Common Market (CARICOM) development of ICH tourism projects for local communities (Jordan and Jolliffe 2013). Similarly, in the Dali region of Yunnan, China, local ethnic women produce traditional tie-dyed cloth as one of their intangible heritage practices to facilitate heritage conservation and local poverty alleviation (Doorne, Ateljevic and Bai 2003). These women strengthen their roles in the local economy and community building through such heritage projects. The local-made cultural products have been sold to tourists and in foreign markets such as New Zealand.

Although ICH opens up possibilities for communities to promote their cultural traditions, the practical and theoretical utility of ICH is still questionable. The officially recognised intangible heritage is often recategorised, decontextualised and displayed for the public in tourism development. Through this process, the listing of traditional practices and expressions contributes to the 'folklorisation' in which cultural practices are frozen in time and space as exotic spectacles for consumption (Hafstein 2004). Cultural performances and festivals, traditionally celebrated only by locals, become a tool to popularise the area for tourism (Richards 2007). As previously mentioned, such transformation is a response to tourists' enthusiasm for authenticity, even though this is not the original intention of the Convention.

Furthermore, despite UNESCO's initial design and focus on community and the distinction between 'the use of heritage for commercial purposes and internal activities of communities' (Aikawa-Faure 2009, 26), the issue of commercialisation becomes evident in the tourism context. It is quite common to promote and stimulate the fetishism of tangible products to legitimise the value of ICH. Rituals, performances, dance and music are recorded and turned into products such as souvenirs, guidebooks, documentaries and historical re-enactments. These cultural practices become resources for commercialisation through the recognition and legitimisation of the heritage discourse (Tunbridge and Ashworth 1996, chapter 1). Consequently, cultural specialists, after being recognised as intangible heritage inheritors, become performers for tourists.

Popular cultural practices have been turned into a nationwide cultural industry in China through the implementation of China's ICH national list (a domestic cultural recognition mechanism). Related professionals create a standard version of heritage to shape new knowledge transmission. The designation of particular cultural practices and practitioners as ICH facilitates social fragmentation, especially in ethnic minority areas. While recognising specific culture has often resulted in more resources for branding and promoting, unlisted cultures rarely survive in the tourism industry market. The struggle for recognition and support has turned this exercise into a local power game (Zhu and Maags 2020).

Figure 13 Intangible cultural heritage display in Yan'an, China

Why do good intentions of designing new approaches to recognise cultural diversity not necessarily lead to expected outcomes? I discuss these reasons in the latter part of this section. For now, however, it is worth noting that the dichotomy between the tangible and intangible is artificial and arbitrary because, under most circumstances, it is impossible to separate practices from material culture. As Smith and Akagawa (2009) note, 'the [Convention] is revealing about the tensions that exist between the different philosophical and conceptual constructs that underpin dominant and author-ised definitions of "heritage", which we might now label "tangible heritage" and "intangible heritage"' (4). This tension was based on the discrepancy between only recognising and valuing the intangible heritage deemed 'out-standing' and 'excellent', or following a more egalitarian approach that would identify the value of all cultural practices. The separation of ICH from material culture merely perpetuates the misrecognition of cultural practices and traditions from physical objects and spaces. In other words, the Convention has only reorganised the World Heritage categories, and has not in fact significantly overhauled how heritage should be understood. As Smith (2006) argues, all heritage is intangible due to the valuation awarded to cultural works and heritage within societies.

Cultural Landscape and Indigenous Tourism

As part of the negotiation of heritage in recognising the diversity of culture, scholars created the idea of the cultural landscape in the 1980s as a way to recognise its connection to conservation and cultural heritage management. Initially used by Friedrich Ratzel in the early twentieth century, the term 'cultural landscape' was an essential concept within geography (notably by Carl Sauer, founding chair of the geography department at the University of California, Berkeley). From the 1960s, 'landscape' became integrated into other disciplines and became an essential term in environmental management and heritage recognition. Within this latter adoption, 'cultural landscape' influenced the cultural and natural definitions of heritage, combining the two distinctions. Thus, the notion of cultural landscape evolved from simply a place or product, to a process in which they are created as a reflection of values, aspirations and histories (Lewis 1979, 12).

This movement led to UNESCO's 1992 revision of the operational guidelines to allow cultural landscapes to be recognised and protected under the 1972 WHC. It defined cultural landscape as embracing 'a diversity of manifestations of the interaction between humankind and its natural environment'. It also put forward three types of cultural landscapes: 'a) clearly defined landscapes designed and created intentionally by man, b) organically evolved landscapes (with two sub-categories: relic or fossil landscapes and continuing landscapes), and c) the associative cultural landscapes' (UNESCO 1992, 4–5).

The adoption of cultural landscapes had important implications in shifting and broadening the definition of heritage promoted by UNESCO; it contributed to the empowerment of indigenous people in a postcolonial era. Indeed, the first two cultural landscapes inscribed on the UNESCO World Heritage List (Tongariro National Park in New Zealand in 1993, and Uluru-Kata Tjuta National Park in Australia in 1994) represent a significant milestone for the indigenous people of those countries (Rössler 1995). Initially, both Tongariro National Park (in 1990) and Uluru National Park (in 1987) were inscribed on the World Heritage List as 'natural' heritage sites, provoking criticism of the UNESCO WHC model and the separation and dualistic opposition of cultural and natural heritage. This criticism led to the 1992 revisions to the World Heritage Operational Guidelines and recognition of the indigenous values of cultural landscapes. As a result of the complex social and physical networks demonstrated by their indigenous custodians, these landscapes should be viewed as exhibiting forms of agency that have had a 'long-lasting impact on how heritage is defined and managed' in the contemporary world (Harrison 2013, 127).

By adopting the concept of cultural landscape and promoting indigenous tourism movements, indigenous communities' roles in heritage management, policymaking and tourism development are increasingly recognised. Such development imbues landscapes with values and images essential to indigenous groups, rather than creating a stereotypical tourism-oriented space. In this way, heritage becomes intertwined with the lives of the people who share its space. The recognition of cultural landscape enables an ongoing relationship between nature and culture that facilitates conservation and ecosystem awareness.

Moreover, cultural landscapes in a heritage tourism context endow local communities with the rights to manage and control tourism resources. Bunten and Graburn (2018) define indigenous tourism as 'any service or product that is [a] owned and operated at least in part by an indigenous group and [b] results from a means of exchange with outside guests' (21). This definition provides indigenous self-determination in tourism, while considering sites as important foci for cross-cultural exchange between consumers and providers (Bunten and Graburn 2018, 2).

Branded as a sacred cultural landscape, Uluru (formerly known as Ayers Rock) in Australia attracted thirty-five thousand non-Australian visitors per year. Many tourists climbed the monolith as part of their tour experience – an act the Anangu communities have discouraged since the 1980s (Shackley

2004). In the 1990s, the Anangu communities introduced a 'Please don't climb' programme out of respect for its spiritual significance to the Anangu people – the route being important to ancestral Mala men on their arrival at Uluru. The programme adopted the idea of *Tjukurpa* (Dreamtime), which refers to the foundation of the life and society of the Anangu. *Tjukurpa* illustrates the relationships between humans, animals, plants and the environment, the relationship between past and present, and the methods for maintaining these relationships in the future. It represents the coherent landscape-centred ontology of the Anangu people at Uluru-Kata Tjuta National Park and a holistic philosophy that now forms the basis for park management (Shackley 2004). As a result, the numbers of climbers declined significantly. Climbing has been banned since October 2019, and more importantly, the programme improved cultural awareness of indigenous values.

Similar to ICH, the implementation of cultural landscapes has also met significant challenges. The 2002 Budapest Declaration on World Heritage considered four 'Cs' (Credibility, Conservation, Capacity building, Communication) in clarifying the meanings and functions of cultural landscape. However, it failed to consider the importance of community for indigenous groups. This issue was particularly evident in countries like New Zealand and Vanuatu where indigenous groups are politically autonomous or significantly recognised (Wilson et al. 2012, 2).

Considering this oversight, 'community' was added to this list as an overarching concept of cultural landscape (Wilson et al. 2012). Local community-based tourism projects have been developed in these areas. In Chief Roi Mata's Domain, a continuing cultural landscape in Vanuatu, the local community has developed 'the Roi Mata Cultural Tours'. This form of community-driven enterprise may be less profitable economically, but it enables sustainable community engagement and the continuation of community-driven culture (Wilson, Ballard and Kalotiti 2011, 10).

Another challenge of promoting cultural landscapes for indigenous tourism is understanding indigeneity in planning and management. In the epilogue of the volume *Indigenous Tourism Movement*, Graburn (2018) considered that the term 'indigeneity' itself is a product of colonialism by Anglophone peoples in the twentieth century. The colonial-influenced Western constructions of the term perpetuated an 'us/them' framework that often has ulterior implications in different parts of the world such as Asia, North America, Australia and Europe. In this sense, we should not solidify the 'exotic other' paradigm when integrating cultural landscape in indigenous tourism (Graburn 2018, 250). Rather than providing a single expertise view of a general understanding of 'indigenous', it is important to acknowledge the meanings of indigeneity from a local perspective. Consultation with local communities is needed to recognise and understand the complexity of the local context as a significant component in heritage interpretation; a topic illustrated in the next section.

Ecomuseums and Community Tourism

In addition to intangible heritage and cultural landscapes, ecomuseums are another instrument developed in recent decades. The conceptual emergence of ecomuseums is part of the development of 'new museology' in the 1970s. Traditional museums were collections-focused, building-based institutions. In contrast to the narrow focus of museums, the new museology advocated a democratised (non-elitist or exclusionary) role for museums within society (Ross 2015). The primary aim is to achieve cultural recognition and empowerment within the heritage, museum and tourism industry (Howard 2002).

In the 1970s, Georges Henri Rivière and Hugues de Varine developed ecomuseums (*écomusée*) in France, emphasising this non-exclusionary and non-elitist role of museums. Unlike traditional museums that have frequently favoured high culture, the ecomuseum (*écomusée*) showcases holistic interpretations of cultural heritage and the significance of 'common' culture. It shifts from a focus on items and objects of social elites to local and daily life (Borrelli and Davis 2012, 33).

Since the 1970s, the concept of the ecomuseum has evolved further as community-heritage projects to promote community participation. Unlike traditional museums bounded by physical space (buildings), ecomuseums are, according to Davis, 'a community-based museum or heritage project that supports sustainable development' (Davis 2007, 199). Such a definition represents a shift from cultural elitism of the few to the democratisation of cultural heritage owned by the community (Davis 2004, 93–4).

Empowerment is a key issue that reflects such changes in museology. As shown earlier, empowerment is understood as giving local special interest groups stewardship over their cultural and natural heritage (Borrelli and Davis 2012, 42). Reflecting on ecomuseum practices in various countries (see Davis 2007), these institutions guide local communities to interpret, preserve, promote or exhibit their cultural and natural heritage. As a critical factor of empowerment, community participation plays a critical role in the development of ecomuseums. The inclusion of local actors in the decision-making process is necessary for drawing on certain cultural and historical knowledge that may otherwise be left out. Moreover, the inclusion of local communities provides more long-lasting results (Borrelli and Davis 2012). It helps to improve self-determination and social recognition (Jamal 2019, 80).

Nowadays, more than four hundred ecomuseums exist worldwide, reflecting their growing importance in articulating and representing community cultural heritage (Davis 2008). Ha Long Bay Ecomuseum in Vietnam provides a setting and opportunities for the local fishing community to participate in developing its natural and cultural assets. Near Valencia, Spain, the Ecomuseu Val Vernissa established the so-called Catalog de Patrimoni (Heritage List) – an agreement to encourage local farmers, producers and inhabitants to take care of their heritage and to make it available to the rest of the community (Borrelli and Davis 2012, 37–40). Similarly, through cooperation between Chinese cultural institutions and the Norwegian government in 1997, four ecomuseums were established in Guizhou Province, including the Buyi Zhengshan Museum and the Suoga Miao Ecomuseum (Graburn and Jin 2017, 21–7). These museums contain oral histories of ethnic minority groups that document their collective memories.

Ecomuseums are not standardised; variation in construction and management can be significant. The Kalyna Ecomuseum in Canada is thousands of square kilometres in size, while the Hemp Ecomuseum in Carmagnolia, Italy is only a few square metres in size (Davis 2008). While some ecomuseums are privately managed (11 per cent), many of them (about 43 per cent) are publicly owned, such as those created by national park authorities or local governments. Volunteers often play a significant role in their management (Borrelli and Davis 2012, 34–5).

The development of ecomuseums often closely aligns with the initiative of 'community tourism'. Unlike external tourism operators, ecomuseums provide local communities a solid platform on which to develop their tourism business. Created by local, traditional and indigenous communities, ecomuseum-led tourism initiatives aim to use local business activities to recognise and protect their cultural and natural resources. Profits should not be the only purpose of such tourism activities; instead, it is about preserving and recognising the sense of place and landscape, and the history of the people who live there. In this sense, community tourism is not a product, but a process aligned with ecomuseums' development.

The creation of ecomuseums and the development of community tourism often encounter challenges within the processes of localisation of international policies, where multiple interest groups compete. Due to the democratised foundation of ecomuseums, the ways they are presented and publicised can differ greatly. This is particularly concerning for local groups, where their involvement in this process has often been debated within ecomuseology, notably how to create a participatory approach and how to develop and negotiate the management of places (Nitzky 2012). In addition, ecomuseum projects might lack sustainable management due to inconsistent funding and resources.

Figure 14 Ecomusée de Colombire in Sion, Switzerland

As Davis (2004) illustrated through studying three different ecomuseums in Japan, even democratised projects require the formalisation of leadership positions within local communities. When leadership changes occur, relationships with the local communities as one of the ecomuseum's critical features may suffer severely (Howard 2002).

Discussion: Empowerment and Challenges

In this section, various instruments (intangible heritage, cultural landscape and ecomuseum) developed by international organisations at similar periods recognise local cultural traditions and resources to promote heritage tourism. Such empowerment can be seen as the global approach of democracy for local capacity building. These new developments can also be regarded as responses to the broader challenges of global heritage tourism indicated in the previous section, such as inequality, exploitation and displacement.

These instruments have three commonalities in terms of their roles of empowerment. First is political empowerment. These instruments endeavour to include marginalised people such as ethnic and indigenous minorities in the capitalistic tourism industry. Second is social empowerment. Rather than focusing on external politicians and experts, all instruments aim at recognising local communities and practitioners as the owners and representatives of their cultural heritage. Third is economic empowerment. When local communities have the capacity to develop heritage tourism, the financial benefit can be shared with their community networks. Combining these three factors of developing heritage tourism can contribute to the improvement of local communities' leadership, social networks and well-being (Lyons, Smuts and Stephens 2001; Simpson, Wood and Daws 2003, 278; Timothy 2007).

However, as we saw from various examples in the heritage tourism context, these international instruments confront similar challenges in policy implementation on the ground. Here I illustrate three factors that lead to these challenges. First is the mechanism of international policymaking. Although these cultural policies integrate democratic approaches for inclusion and diversity, they are still limited to the existing international organisation structures. Some of them, such as cultural landscape and ecomuseum, are scholarly concepts adapted to international policies. Others, such as intangible heritage, developed within UNESCO with support from state parties and advisory bodies. The procedure of policymaking in general still follows a top-down approach; the voices from actual practitioners are difficult to reach for international organisations mostly situated in Europe.

This is not to say that international organisations do not intend to include ideas from cultural practitioners. The ICH Convention has gone through various stages of discussion via meetings and workshops that include heritage and tourism practitioners from many countries around the world. However, the best practices, collected from local heritage sites through emails and site workshops, are difficult to develop into a collective vision that shapes the professional version of international policies. The results of meetings and collected case studies eventually lead to publications and promotional materials; their actual impacts on policymaking are nonetheless questionable.

Second is the mechanism of international policy transfer. 'Policy transfer' – discussed widely by political scientists and international relations scholars – focuses on patterns that lead to success and failure of policy implementation (e.g. Benson and Jordan 2011). As World Heritage and ICH status are often closely associated with state parties' interests, the implementation of international instruments in local heritage tourism projects is still based on the capacity of NGOs such as UNESCO regional offices, and the interests of the associated state parties.

Thus, the critical factors of policy transfer are (a) the existing power structures within nation states and (b) the interaction between international policies and local traditional bureaucratic culture. Without proper mediation among international organisations, nation states and local communities, these instruments and policies might become another tool to legitimize national and local governments' political and economic agendas. They can sometimes even create new problems of maldistribution and misrecognition.

In China, the party-state has integrated global heritage and tourism concepts and value systems into its national political system (Zhu and Maags 2020). China's hierarchical power structure gives agency to official heritage institutions to appropriate international concepts on the national and lower scales. As part of the mechanism of policy transfer, the national heritage and tourism administration often organises training workshops on a related theme such as 'community participation' or 'sustainable development'. Subsequently, the development of community-based heritage tourism relies heavily on the governance of national and local states. Most of the ecomuseums in China still use a top-down, government-led approach for planning and management (Gan 2009; Nitzky 2012). Once the local governments lose their interest in developing ecomuseums as a branding strategy for the local

Figure 15 The exhibition centre of the Dong Ethnic Minority Ecomuseum in Guizhou, China

tourism industry, these projects cease, leaving the cultural exhibition centres to collapse.

Third is local politics within communities. Heritage tourism often expects a single, simplified image of heritage sites or culture that can be exhibited to external visitors. However, disparity often exists within communities due to differences in class, gender, generation and profession. The implementation of cultural policies for heritage tourism is not only driven by the interaction between external stakeholders and communities, but also closely associated with the power dimension within communities.

When designing heritage tourism, empowerment approaches should not take 'community' as a comfortable, fixed label or a form of 'box-ticking' for external experts. Ignoring communities' internal political system might legitimate and mask the power of the external stakeholders. Even worse, it might facilitate the development of neoliberal ethics of individualism and reinforce intra-group domination, especially by the wealthy and the powerful. In their examination of several ecomuseums in northern Italy, Corsane et al. (2007) found that, despite the general purpose of the ecomuseums, significant variation can exist due to local contexts and needs. The actual projects of ecomuseums cannot always realise the theorised democratised and community-driven approach. They cannot necessarily resolve, for example, conflicts between conservation and tourism development, between environmental protection and economic interests, or among communities, government officials and developers.

Within the context of heritage tourism, the community consultation concerning intangible heritage, cultural landscape and ecomuseum projects often involves engagement with a spokesperson of the local communities, such as an administrative or religious leader at heritage sites. However, many questions remain within the local politics of communities: is such a consultation process useful for social recognition of the diverse needs of communities, especially the needs of elders, women and children? Does heritage tourism development allow all community members to interact with one another as peers? Furthermore, can the design of heritage tourism also include voices from tourists and new migrants?

These challenges have no simple answers. All of these questions should be considered during policy implementation to accommodate the full complexity of the internal policies of communities. We need to rethink the power dimension of heritage tourism and find a way to solve – or at least mitigate – the problems and challenges raised from the heritage tourism industry. One way to tackle these issues is through co-production, which I discuss in detail next.

5 Co-production

In the previous two sections, I discussed the mechanisms involved in global heritage tourism and the social, economic and political impacts on heritage sites and associated communities. International organisations have developed various instruments to acknowledge and build up awareness of communities' involvement in designing, planning and managing heritage tourism. Many scholars have addressed the importance of the participatory approach in heritage tourism associated with social equity, environmental resilience and cultural preservation (Timothy 1999). However, challenges arise on the ground in terms of policy transfer and implementation.

Heritage tourism needs to apply integrated and holistic approaches that incorporate the complex dynamics of the local-global scale within the tourism industry. More precisely, I suggest that heritage tourism should be treated as a form of co-production: a mechanism of community-centred governance that integrates recognition and interpretation to advance dialogue, equity and diversity.

'Co-production' is defined here as a local institutional mechanism of collaborative and cooperative work associated with various stages of heritage tourism. In co-production, all stakeholders at heritage sites – including experts and non-experts – should be integrated into the planning, design, interpretation and management process. Furthermore, co-production emphasises equity rather than equality. Community is situated at the centre of heritage tourism governance. Otherwise, co-production might become another official slogan of citizen engagement and local participation.

This section illustrates various elements of heritage tourism as co-production. As the complexity of heritage tourism often varies depending on social and political contexts, the discussion here does not intend to offer universal solutions to these global challenges. Instead, the proposal serves as cultural guidance to avoid problems similar to those discussed in the previous sections.

Collaborative Governance

The first and most important task is to ensure that the local political environment can facilitate the co-production of heritage tourism. Local governments often provide the most decisive input into the development of the tourism industry at heritage sites. However, co-production needs to shift away from the traditional hierarchical structure of governance towards collaborative networks and the involvement of communities. Co-production requires local collaborative governance that contributes to the development of more sustainable forms of tourism. It is a process whereby different parties see problems and work together to find solutions that may have been beyond an individual's original purview (Gray 1989, 5). According to Timothy and Tosun (2003), five main agencies are involved in productive collaboration in heritage tourism: (1) government agencies, (2) the private and public sectors, (3) different levels of administration, (4) same-level administrations and (5) private-sector services.

Among these forms of collaborative governance, local community-based civil societies should be situated at the centre of co-production. In the heritage tourism context, the term 'civil society' refers to cultural institutions organised by local communities. These groups defend local interests as well as specific values against or beyond official political influence. The critical factor for success is the degree to which local groups and individuals can control cultural resources. In this way, they can mediate different value systems among stakeholders within and outside the communities as part of decision-making and planning (Wergin 2012). Such an institutional mechanism allows local communities to benefit socially, culturally and economically from the tourism industry.

Let us revisit the notion of empowerment discussed in the previous section. Dallen Timothy (2007) proposed four types of empowerment depending on the degree of local control in cultural resources management and decision-making: (1) imposed development, (2) tokenistic involvement, (3) meaningful participation and (4) true empowerment. According to Timothy's (2007) model, an acceptable form of 'true empowerment' can be achieved when local communities have full ownership of and responsibility for their cultural resources. Empowerment of local communities is evident in the designing of heritage programmes in Maori meeting houses in New Zealand. Maori elders protect and sustain their cultural and spiritual materials while inviting external heritage professionals to participate in the restoration work. In this situation, the Maori elders have the authority to renew traditional arts and collections and decide what should be cleansed (Stovel 2005).

Concurrently, local states should not treat these community-based civil societies as a threat to their interests. Instead, a dialogical relationship between local states and civil societies could be established at all stages of heritage tourism. In some authoritarian countries where central and local states take charge of cultural resources and landownership of heritage sites, co-production of heritage tourism encourages central and local states to develop cultural policies and awareness training to support community-based activities. In addition, regular monitoring mechanisms and checks and balances could be developed at the local level to avoid heritage tourism becoming merely a profit-focused project. The involvement of an internal auditing system and external public media could avoid the monopoly of cultural resources and collective corruption.

In addition to these instruments, three elements could be considered as the foundation of co-production despite the complexities of the local context. First, different stakeholders have genuine motivations to collaborate in developing heritage tourism. Second, they are willing to give up specific interests to develop mutual understandings. Third, a good communication strategy can create consensus and solutions. These three elements combine to provide a 'quality of life and level of sustainability as seen by members of that community' (Beeton 2006, 80). Essential to these elements are the linkages between community well-being (economic success, acceptance of otherness, sense of belonging) and a supportive environment for maintaining connections.

Recognition, Redistribution and Social Justice

Once a mechanism for local collaborative governance is established, co-production in heritage tourism requires adopting political lenses that address diversity among social groups at heritage sites. Here Nancy Fraser's (2001, 2003) discussion on the politics of recognition is useful to illustrate emancipation and justice in the heritage tourism industry.

In Fraser's discussion, recognition is not just a management issue: it is a matter of politics and social justice to ensure the rights of diverse groups in public policy development and implementation. Fraser's (2003) idea of 'parity of participation' aims to ensure that all group members can participate in social interactions as peers. This concept has often been applied to global social movements associated with inequality and misrecognition, such as Black Lives Matter or LGBT politics.

Engagement with the politics of recognition and social justice is also fundamental in co-producing heritage tourism, particularly for mediating the relationship between global tourism consumption and local heritage values (Jamal 2019). As cultural injustice is deeply 'rooted in social patterns of representation, interpretation and communication' (Fraser 2003, 13), ownership of cultural heritage has become the core matter in applying Fraser's discussion of 'parity of participation'. The questions behind the discussion are who owns heritage, and how they should be involved in the production and management of the heritage tourism industry.

Following Fraser (2003)'s discussion of recognition, several questions need to be considered in the ethics and justice of heritage tourism (Jamal 2019). These questions include how fair the institutional arrangement of heritage tourism is for social interaction among different stakeholders. Does the development of heritage tourism advantage or disadvantage certain groups or communities connected to heritage sites? Does heritage tourism create or reinforce status hierarchy and social stratification? Does the design include all members of the community such as elders, women and youth? Further, should 'parity of participation' only apply to long-term, permanent members of communities, or should it also include the rights and needs of migrants and visitors at heritage sites?

Discussing these questions might not solve the problems of misrecognition in heritage tourism. However, cultural recognition and the politics of difference in tourism can create shared social spaces that embrace hospitality while developing an ethics of care for the other in host-guest encounters (Jamal 2019, 220). In this way, social and cultural rights of both hosts and guests can be recognised and respected.

Continuing with Fraser's model (2003, 63), redistribution is another component of social justice and should not be separated from recognition. Both approaches must be considered together to achieve social and cultural equality. Accordingly, it is essential to note that culture and economy should not be separated within the heritage tourism context. In other words, identity politics and economic distribution of social goods should work together instead of in two separate domains. These two issues should be integrated to design heritage tourism projects that focus on generating resources for local capacity building and community well-being. Such integration would allow different social groups to participate in heritage tourism's policy and planning process while accessing and utilising cultural and economic resources to enhance their lives collectively (Fraser 2003).

As shown in the previous sections, maldistribution of economic profit has always been a key challenge in heritage tourism, especially in developing countries where external enterprises dominate the tourism market. Therefore, a key element of co-producing heritage tourism is to develop a platform of profit and resource redistribution within communities of heritage sites. In designing the platform of redistribution, similar questions of the politics of recognition can be considered to avoid social stratification and maldistribution. Questions could include: How can resources and profits from heritage tourism be fairly distributed within communities of heritage sites? Are the needs of elders, women and children recognised within resource sharing? How about members working and staying outside of heritage sites and tourism businesses? What about tourism migrant workers? What position do these groups have within the redistribution of profit and resources?

These questions of redistribution have no universal solution because all issues need to be embedded in local political contexts. In some villages in China, when the mechanism of profits redistribution has been developed for the tourism industry, people from other places become motivated to move into these villages through marriage arrangements in order to share profits and resources. Thus, the issue of the rights of new members arises in this process of redistribution. Again, there is no fixed pattern for the mechanism of resources redistribution to solve these problems. Instead, they are questions that need to be frequently revisited as a regular agenda of co-production. In so doing, the power dynamics of the heritage tourism industry and its impacts on local societies can be fully considered.

Above all, recognition and redistribution are two significant components of co-producing heritage tourism. Engagement with the politics of recognition and redistribution facilitates emancipation and social justice in the processes of heritage tourism management. They do not merely aim at consensus making, but rather work to develop a practical and dialogical mechanism for all stake-holders to participate in the co-production of heritage tourism.

Heritage Interpretation in Co-production

Another important task of heritage tourism lies in 'reconstructing the past in the present through interpretation' (Nuryanti 1996, 252). Heritage interpretation is one of the critical issues in linking global standards and local uniqueness in heritage tourism. A critical task for co-production is to develop strategies that help tourists to understand and appreciate others' cultural heritage.

Local states often play essential roles in heritage interpretation as they provide funding and resources to support the official production of heritage interpretation. However, official versions of heritage interpretation led by experts and professionals might not satisfy tourists, as they often provide 'a single, monolithic interpretation supporting a particular ideological frame-work' (Poria, Biran and Reichel 2009, 94). Therefore, heritage interpretation should not be carried out only by officials but instead should be a co-production among external organisations, local communities, tour guides and visitors.

Among different heritage interpretation techniques such as brochures, films, and music, interactive engagement was the most successful form of engaging tourists on an informative and emotional level (Io 2013). Tour guides, especially from local communities, do not merely communicate factual information; instead, they can often enhance tourists' experience by sharing personal stories, experiences and unique cultural insights (Zeppel and Muloin 2008).

In 2005, a local heritage tour guide training programme was set up by the UNESCO Office in Bangkok and the UNESCO-ICCROM Asian Academy for Heritage Management (Salazar and Zhu 2015). This programme was designed as an integrative and collaborative initiative between various ministries and organisations, providing important guidelines and knowledge for heritage con-servation and sustainability. This programme has seen much success, having been implemented in several Asian countries, including Thailand, India and

Indonesia. From a 2011 launch in Vietnam, approximately twenty participants received training on identifying and managing local heritage (Salazar and Zhu 2015, 252).

Traditionally, tour guides serve as instructors, information providers, leaders, translators and companions (Cohen 1985; Reisinger and Steiner 2006; Scherle and Nonnenmann 2008). In the context of heritage interpretation, tour guides become facilitators in mediating the connection between physical heritage sites, the built environment and cultural meaning. They guide visitors to see beyond materiality and experience meanings behind heritage sites' physical settings. In addition to meaning-making, heritage interpretation helps tourists understand conservation, sustainability and, importantly, respect for heritage sites (Moscardo 1996). It is not a straightforward matter of education and signage, but 'entails complex negotiation between guides' self-positioning, that of their organisation, the particular genre of tourism involved, the audience and the site itself' (Macdonald 2006, 136).

Furthermore, heritage interpretation should also include local communities surrounding heritage sites as part of co-production (Silberman 2012). In detail, members of local communities, regardless of their gender and age, can be invited by the tourism managers to participate in designing and interpreting materials to tell their own stories to visitors. This form of co-producing heritage

Figure 16 City heritage tour in Madrid, Spain

interpretation provides these groups with opportunities to link their cultural tradition and personal life experience; thus strengthening their cultural identity and sense of belonging. This issue is particularly relevant to heritage tourism in aboriginal areas where indigenous communities and their culture are situated at the centre of heritage interpretation. In this way, the representation and interpretation of local history, knowledge and environment can follow the indigenous ontological vision of the world beyond Western philosophies, such as the division between nature and culture, and tangible and intangible (Wergin 2016).

By extension, visitors can participate in heritage interpretation through presenting their unique travel experiences at heritage sites. Visitors are not passive information receivers (Sliberman 2012); they can actively record their understanding of heritage values by engaging with visitors' books and online social media. These records are integrated as part of the authentic and valuable interpretation of heritage sites. In this way, interpretation raises heritage tourism to a broader platform to 'enhance understanding, appreciation, and protection of cultural and natural legacy' (Beck and Cable 2002, 1).

Above all, all participants – local states, local tour guides, local communities, visitors and international organisations – would be seen as potential co-producers in heritage interpretation. Here co-production breaks the relationship between consumers and producers. All participants are viewed as collaborators and dialogical partners. Viewing heritage interpretation as co-production shifts the focus of interpretation from information and knowledge production to the mediation of dialogues between different people in heritage tourism settings.

The Ladder of Heritage Interpretation

Once the local mechanisms of collaborative governance, recognition, redistribution and interpretation have been established, heritage tourism goes beyond a form of consumption, entertainment and knowledge sharing. Instead, it can contribute to society in more meaningful ways, such as acknowledging and contending with racial differences, enabling the empowerment of minority groups and providing self-determination and self-worth in community building (Barton and Leonard 2010). Here, a typology of five levels of heritage interpretation can elaborate the various social functions embedded within heritage tourism co-production (Figure 17). For illustrative purposes, these five types are arranged in a ladder pattern, with each step corresponding visitor interaction with heritage sites and associated communities.

On the first step of the ladder, heritage interpretation contributes to visitor entertainment and consumption. Unlike knowledge sharing and recognition, heritage tourism at this stage serves hedonistic pleasure seeking as its primary

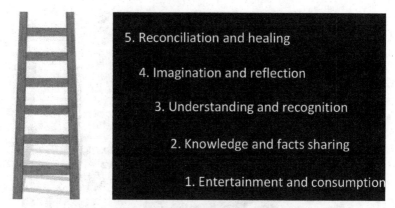

Figure 17 The ladder of heritage interpretation

purpose. Visitor consumption at some historical re-enactment sites becomes romanticised as a form of commoditised production. In this scenario, visitors might not be interested in the historical facts of the past. Instead, visitors are attracted by a romanticised performance that serves their hedonistic desire for experiencing others (Zhu 2018b). The first step can also refer to dark heritage sites where visitors are attracted by the atmosphere without recognising the actual meanings and history of the site.

The second step of the ladder is knowledge and fact sharing. This step is often associated with official heritage descriptions and narratives made by experts and professionals. Such official information typically incorporates historical backgrounds of heritage sites through a chronological order that includes specific years, dates and events associated with the sites. This type of information is presented as factual, unemotional and objective.

The third step of heritage interpretation offers a deeper level of understanding and recognition. This stage provides answers to why and how certain historical events took place. As seen in the example of the comfort women museum in Nanjing (Figure 18), the statue itself became a form of heritage interpretation that acknowledges the event's traumatic nature and its impact on affected communities. At this stage, recognition becomes a powerful cultural practice to establish the relationship between the host community and visitors (Macdonald 2013).

Through commemorative practices and rituals, heritage interpretation allows tourism engagement to (re)construct narratives of cultural connection between visitors and host communities. The issue of recognition in heritage tourism is particularly relevant to visitors whose families have personal connections with those heritage sites. Transylvanian Saxons and their descendants develop a sense of transnational community by visiting Romania's heritage sites such as public monuments, memorial plaques and exhibitions from Germany (Iorio

Figure 18 Comfort women museum in Nanjing, China

and Corsale 2013). Such visits can offer 'spiritual truth, emotional response, deeper meaning and understanding' (Nuryanti 1996, 253).

The fourth step of heritage interpretation is about imagination and reflection. Unlike the previous stages that concerned facts and knowledge, this step enables visitors to traverse the boundaries between heritage and memory. At one of the spaces in the Jewish Museum in Berlin, phrased as *Shalekhet* (Fallen Leaves), more than ten thousand heavy round iron plates cut in the form of faces with crying mouths cover the empty space. Instead of presenting factual truth, this form of artistic interpretation of history highlights the emotional connection between visitors and the site. It engages with narratives and affects that make people feel rather than understand (Smith, Wetherell and Campbell 2018).

Narratives are one of the key strategies in heritage interpretation. As Russell Staiff (2016, 113) argues, narrative makes 'material things the touchstone of our deepest desires, feelings, imaginations and emotions'. Storytelling is another powerful way of connecting people to places and landscapes, offering imagination and the possibility of transcending the present towards the past and future. Instead of being driven by experts, stories need to be developed through co-production and dialogical interaction among local communities.

The last step presents heritage tourism with an opportunity for healing and reconciliation. As a result of co-production, heritage tourism could be used as a spiritual space of healing for those people or their family members who experienced cultural trauma and loss. A good example is the Hiroshima Peace Memorial Park in Japan or Kigali Genocide Memorial in Rwanda. Such visits also have the potential for reconciliation within divided societies, fostering peace and reducing conflicts between different groups (Barton and Leonard 2010).

These social functions of heritage tourism are particularly relevant to post-conflict and dark heritage sites associated with tragic events or human suffering such as jails, concentration camps, battlefields, war memorials and cemeteries. Scholars, officials, victims and their family members can be invited to discuss

Figure 19 Heritage tour at the Australian War Memorial, Australia

their interpretation of the site and its associated past. Questions include: How did the event(s) occur? How have people suffered? How have such issues been recognised and settled? Most importantly, how can we learn from the past to create a better future without making similar mistakes?

Incorporating these questions in heritage interpretation is particularly important when engaging with crucial and hidden knowledge of the dark past. The Kigali Genocide Memorial provides a transparent acceptance and recognition of the Rwandan genocide and the devastating impact one ethnic group had on another (Sodaro 2011). Similarly, Hiroshima has been reconstructed as a 'City of Bright Peace' through memorials and tourism to commemorate the atomic bombings in the context of World War II (Zwigenberg 2014). Reconciliation is also a critical sociopolitical and cultural agenda in Australia. Many Aboriginal

Figure 20 Peace guide with students at Nagasaki, Japan

art festivals and programmes recognise the importance of reconciling indigenous and non-indigenous differences and histories (Higgins-Desbiolles 2016). One such place of recognition is the Lurujarri heritage trails in North West Australia, which were established as a collaborative project between people and the land to acknowledge different world views and indigenous culture (Wergin 2016).

Reconciliation is a complex and challenging endeavour. It requires all stakeholders to work together – as part of the co-production process – to develop heritage interpretation strategies that acknowledge and prioritise community well-being and the needs of post-conflict societies. Otherwise, the social function of healing and reconciliation can easily fall prey to superficial propaganda without any meaningful impacts on local societies.

Funded by international organisations, the old bridge at Mostar, demolished during the Croat-Bosniak War, was reconstructed and nominated as a World Heritage Site by UNESCO in 2005. The post-war reconstruction of the bridge functions as a powerful emblem of international cooperation and political unification between Bosnia and Herzegovina. However, local recognition of the bridge as a unifying feature between two political powers is limited, resulting in a locally hollow monument devoid of meaning except for official propaganda (Wollentz 2017). Moreover, the official heritage interpretation neglects the local tradition in which the bridge serves as an important place for local celebration (men jumping and diving from the bridge).

The co-production of heritage tourism for healing and reconciliation is a long journey for all related parties, as victims of traumatic events have not yet been recognised in many places due to the complex political situations of relevant nation states. The interpretation of narratives concerning the past, especially those of dark histories, requires an assessment from multiple points of view, thus providing an open dialogue on relationship building, not only between nations, but also between state and society.

While the five-step ladder is a simplification, it illustrates various gradations of heritage interpretation and their contribution to the co-production of heritage tourism. Knowing these gradations makes it possible for all actors to clarify their own goals concerning heritage tourism as it fits with particular local conditions. Efforts targeted towards the higher steps on the ladder, such as healing and reconciliation, are more likely to result in effective acceptance of the past and more collaborative work in the future (MacDonald 2015). In partnership with social media, NGOs, educational scholarship and public engagement, the co-production of heritage tourism can hopefully create a 'dialogic historical literacy' (Saito 2016) to move beyond local or national interests and instead consider the broader impact of the industry with a view to achieving a greater sense of cosmopolitanism.

Trust, Empathy and Resilience in Co-production

So far, I have shown various issues in the framework of heritage tourism as co-production. First, co-production requires a local institutional mechanism of collaborative governance to facilitate the negotiation between various stakeholders. Such a mechanism not only aims at mediating the relationship between the external stakeholders and internal administration; it also serves to reconcile conflicts among internal community members of heritage sites. Second, co-production of heritage tourism engages with cultural recognition and economic redistribution to ensure all community members, especially marginalised groups, can be recognised. Third, co-production of heritage tourism concerns heritage interpretation as a mediating mechanism for dialogue among international organisations, local tour guides, visitors and other members of communities. Fourth, co-production invites all social members, public media and civil societies to engage with the past narratives of heritage sites to support cross-cultural understanding and reconciliation.

Despite the distinct contexts of countries around the world, some observable social factors need to be illustrated to fulfil the goals of co-production. I extend the discussion here to assert that heritage tourism requires certain soft skills for different stakeholders to establish a dialogical relationship in the process of recognition, redistribution and interpretation. These skills include developing social trust, empathy and community resilience.

First, the co-production of heritage tourism requires different stakeholders to work together with mutual trust. Social trust is an ongoing base of social relationships. Without trust, the legitimacy of certain groups is undermined, so too communication and understanding between groups and individuals.

Within a heritage tourism context, social trust enables an open dialogue between various stakeholders through which to interpret heritage values and determine key information. The benefits of trust extend beyond the breakdown of asymmetrical power relationships, notably in the form of improved and equitable decision-making and increased community participation. It contributes to the development of a more horizontal or equal relationship between experts and non-experts.

Second, co-production requires people to develop empathy, especially in recognising and interpreting cultural values. According to Pedwell (2012), empathy is 'an important ingredient of affirmative social transformation which recognises and respects the subjectivity and agency of others' (165–6). In other words, empathy provides a mechanism for the revelation of inequalities between various stakeholders and a pathway for alleviating this disparity.

Within the tourism industry, empathy plays an essential role in the communication of ideas and values between host and guest (Tucker 2016). This issue is especially pertinent for post-conflict sites that require cross-cultural learning and mutual understanding. Empathy is vital in contexts such as slavery museums that need to present their stories in an empathetic manner, allowing visitors from different cultural backgrounds to understand the problems of 'affective inequality' (Modlin, Alderman and Gentry 2011, 15). Subsequently, empathy provides a powerful mechanism in evaluating social actions and the necessary grounding for reconciliation through heritage tourism. Without empathy, a deep engagement with the past (particularly narratives concerning conflict) cannot be achieved, and heritage interpretation remains at a superficial level without meaning-making.

Third, community resilience can be another critical indicator of social sustainability for internal and external co-producers of heritage tourism. Community resilience initially focuses on vulnerability and adaptability, especially at places with ecological and environmental disasters (Berkes and Ross 2013). In a heritage tourism context, community resilience refers to local communities' capacity to engage with the dramatic influx of external capital, people and information into heritage sites. These external influences can sometimes be positive (such as increasing social welfare) or negative (such as reinforcing local inequality, conflict and social stratification). Therefore, community resilience can be integrated into the co-production of heritage tourism to review the local capacity of engaging with and recovering from those dramatic changes.

When measuring the external influences of heritage tourism, local heritage managers sometimes treat those changes as a threat to communities. The 'threat-based' paradigm is often driven by the larger 'heritage at risk' framework that focuses on physical vulnerability against external negative influences (Holtorf 2015; Rico 2016). Such a dominant discourse often neglects the fact that communities and their cultural heritage constantly change and evolve. Therefore, co-production should consider integrating those ever-changing traditional knowledge and cultural practices into heritage tourism projects to increase community resilience. In so doing, heritage tourism shifts from being a threat to something that gives social and cultural support.

Above all, social trust, empathy and community resilience could be integrated to facilitate the co-production of heritage tourism. In practice, all stakeholders can review the following questions when co-producing heritage tourism. Socially, can heritage tourism help build local social networks and generate a sense of belonging to confront the influx of visitors? Culturally, can heritage tourism assist in promoting community practices such as rituals and cultural festivals to enhance community resilience? Additionally, can the local society develop a financial system to manage the economic flow from the tourism industry and strengthen its future risk management? By integrating these questions into the process of governance, recognition and interpretation, co-production of heritage tourism can be achieved, allowing local communities to embrace both internal and external disturbances through cross-cultural learning and tourism encounters (Holtorf 2018).

6 Future of Heritage Tourism

This research uses a critical interdisciplinary approach to examine the social, political and economic impacts of tourism on heritage sites and their associated communities. It focuses on criticising the hegemonic power of global systems, the ghosts of colonialism and neoliberal structures and their influences on societies. Heritage tourism should not only be treated as a management and business issue; it is also a political project. The political framework of heritage tourism includes a market-oriented vision controlled by international guidelines, state powers and global economic structures. It is often associated with conflicts, power, legitimacy and political and economic struggles in various parts of the world.

Heritage tourism is also a global ethics project that engages with community well-being and social justice. Local heritage tourism operators play significant roles in shaping the social fabric of heritage sites, especially resource allocation, cultural interpretation and spatial transformation. Mismanaged development of heritage tourism might lead to neoliberal injustice in the forms of economic exploitation and dispossession. The ethical debates here are not only about the ownership of cultural heritage, but also about the issues of social equality and cultural sustainability of local communities. More importantly, the ethics of heritage tourism are closely associated with the well-being and self-determination of communities. In this sense, economic profits and the reputations of heritage sites should not be treated as the only priorities of daily management. Social justice and various forms of rights can be considered through different instruments of empowerment to recognise the different needs of social groups, especially marginalised and minority communities (Jamal 2019, 234).

This research further offers potential channels to mitigate existing challenges and enable emancipation. I have advocated for a holistic and inclusive approach that considers heritage tourism as a form of co-production. The idea of co-production focuses on governance and daily management on the local scale. The dialogical approach of co-production shifts away from the priority of management efficiency and effectiveness in heritage tourism. Instead, it provides a mechanism of community-centred governance that integrates equity, social justice and resilience into the agendas of heritage tourism. This framework repositions heritage tourism to focus on the rights of local communities and their social well-being while offering visitors opportunities to respect and commemorate the past of others.

In 2020–1, the COVID-19 pandemic transformed the world into a new normal. Unlike previous disasters such as the 2004 tsunami in the Indian Ocean and the 2009 swine flu, international and domestic tourism shut down in many parts of the world due to the global crisis. It is yet difficult to predict the long-term impacts of the pandemic on the tourism industry in the post-COVID era; however, two issues need to be addressed for us to rethink and redefine the nature of heritage tourism.

First, the world is experiencing a temporary but possibly long-term process of deglobalisation (Niewiadomski 2020). As a result of travel restrictions (both domestic and international), physical barriers between localities and countries have re-emerged. Regardless of political positions (liberal or conservative), national authorities have used effective mechanisms to control political and economic resources for the purposes of security and domestic stability. Consequently, in both the Global North and South, nation states have become more defensive – as opposed to cooperative – in engaging with natural and cultural disasters on the global stage.

Second, the need has emerged for better digital technologies to connect places and communities virtually. While the digitisation of heritage has been discussed for more than a decade, people have benefited from online heritage and virtual museums during the pandemic lockdown. With UNESCO's acceptance of virtual heritage, digital technologies have been actively adopted in many heritage sectors. Many cultural activities, festivals, religious rituals and heritage programmes have been digitalised. While most international organisations, cultural institutions and the public embrace new technologies, such development poses new challenges for us to rethink how the past is interpreted and imagined. While many people embrace the convenience of digital technology to communicate and explore the world without actually travelling, these new trends include an even more substantial effect of inclusion and exclusion than ever. People who do not have sufficient resources to utilise this digital shift have been marginalised in the new normal. In other words, digitalisation of cultural heritage has emerged as an even more powerful tool to reinforce and legitimise state regulation of class, race or neoliberal ideologies.

Both the trend of deglobalisation and nationalism and the emergence of digital heritage fever will potentially increase social inequality while further disempowering local communities from accessing and utilising cultural and economic resources for their well-being. This new challenge requires us to think further about the nature of heritage tourism and its impacts on local communities, especially minorities and indigenous peoples. We need a more rational view of ethical guidelines to navigate how we interpret the past for the future. While this research is perhaps only a start, a further critical and ethical discussion is needed to review the consequences of heritage tourism on societies. We need to look for practical and critical approaches that guide us in developing community-centred heritage tourism for current and future generations.

Bibliography

Affleck, J., and Kvan, T. (2008) 'A Virtual Community As the Context for Discursive Interpretation: A Role in Cultural Heritage Engagement', *International Journal of Heritage Studies*, 14(3), pp. 268–80.

Aikawa, N. (2004) 'An Historical Overview of the Preparation of the UNESCO International Convention for the Safeguarding of the Intangible Cultural Heritage', *Museum International*, 56(1–2), pp. 137–49.

Aikawa-Faure, N. (2009) 'From the Proclamation of Masterpieces to the Convention for the Safeguarding of Intangible Cultural Heritage', in Smith, L., and Akagawa, N. (eds.), *Intangible Heritage*. Key Issues in Cultural Heritage. London: Routledge, pp. 13–44.

Anderson, B. (1983) *Imagined Communities: Reflections on the Origin and Spread of Nationalism*. London; New York: Verso.

Appadurai, A. (ed.) (1988) *The Social Life of Things: Commodities in Cultural Perspective*. Cambridge: Cambridge University Press.

Ashley, C. (2006) *Participation by the Poor in [the] Luang Prabang Tourism Economy: Current Earnings and Opportunities for Expansion*. London: SNV, ODI, London.

Ashworth, G. J., and Tunbridge, J. E. (1999) 'Old Cities, New Pasts: Heritage Planning in Selected Cities of Central Europe', *GeoJournal*, 49(1), pp. 105–16.

Ateljevic, I., Pritchard, A. and Morgan, N. (eds.) (2007) *The Critical Turn in Tourism Studies*. London; New York: Routledge.

Ball, S. J. (2013) 'Management As Moral Technology: A Luddite Analysis', in Ball, S. J. (ed.), *Foucault and Education: Disciplines and Knowledge*. London; New York: Routledge, pp. 20–32.

Bammer, A. (ed.) (1994) *Displacements: Cultural Identities in Question*. Bloomington: Indiana University Press.

Banaszkiewicz, M., Graburn, N. and Owsianowska, S. (2017) 'Tourism in (Post)Socialist Eastern Europe', *Journal of Tourism and Cultural Change*, 15(2), pp. 109–21.

Barton, A. W., and Leonard, S. J. (2010) 'Incorporating Social Justice in Tourism Planning: Racial Reconciliation and Sustainable Community Development in the Deep South', *Community Development*, 41(3), pp. 298–322.

Beck, L., and Cable, T. T. (2002) *Interpretation for the 21st Century: Fifteen Guiding Principles for Interpreting Nature and Culture*. Champaign, IL: Sagamore.

Beeton, S. (2006) *Community Development through Tourism*. Collingwood, VIC: Land Links.

Benson, D., and Jordan, A. (2011) 'What Have We Learned from Policy Transfer Research? Dolowitz and Marsh Revisited', *Political Studies Review*, 9(3), pp. 366–78.

Berkes, F., and Ross, H. (2013) 'Community Resilience: Toward an Integrated Approach', *Society & Natural Resources*, 26(1), pp. 5–20.

Best, S., and Kellner, D. (1997) *The Postmodern Turn*. New York; London: Guilford Press.

Bianchi, R. V. (2009) 'The "Critical Turn" in Tourism Studies: A Radical Critique', *Tourism Geographies*, 11(4), pp. 484–504.

Bloch, N. (2016) 'Evicting Heritage: Spatial Cleansing and Cultural Legacy at the Hampi UNESCO Site in India', *Critical Asian Studies*, 48(4), pp. 556–78.

Boniface, P., and Fowler, P. J. (1993) *Heritage and Tourism in 'the Global Village'*: New York: Routledge.

Boorstin, D. J. (1964) *The Image: A Guide to Pseudo-events in America*. New York: Harper & Row.

Borrelli, N., and Davis, P. (2012) 'How Culture Shapes Nature: Reflections on Ecomuseum Practices', *Nature and Culture*, 7(1), pp. 31–47.

Bourdeau, L., Gravari-Barbas, M. and Robinson, M. (eds.) (2015) *World Heritage, Tourism and Identity: Inscription and Co-production*. Burlington, VT: Ashgate.

Bourdieu, P. (1984) *Distinction: A Social Critique of the Judgement of Taste*. Translated by R. Nice. Cambridge, MA: Harvard University Press.

Bramwell, B., and Lane, B. (2014) 'The "Critical Turn" and Its Implications for Sustainable Tourism Research', *Journal of Sustainable Tourism*, 22(1), pp. 1–8.

Britton, S. (1982) 'The Political Economy of Tourism in the Third World', *Annals of Tourism Research*, 9(3), pp. 331–58.

Britton, S. (1991) 'Tourism, Capital, and Place: Towards a Critical Geography of Tourism', *Environment and Planning D: Society and Space*, 9(4), pp. 451–78.

Bruner, E. M., and Kirshenblatt-Gimblett, B. (1994) 'Maasai on the Lawn: Tourist Realism in East Africa', *Cultural Anthropology*, 9(4), pp. 435–70.

Bryce, D., Murdy, S. and Alexander, M. (2017) 'Diaspora, Authenticity and the Imagined Past', *Annals of Tourism Research*, 66, pp. 49–60.

Bunten, A. C., and Graburn, N. H. H. (eds.) (2018) *Indigenous Tourism Movements*. Toronto; Buffalo: University of Toronto Press.

Camacho, M. E. M. (1996) 'Dissenting Workers and Social Control: A Case Study of the Hotel Industry in Huatulco, Oaxaca', *Human Organization*, 55(1), pp. 33–40.

Cameron, C. M., and Gatewood, J. B. (2011) 'Beyond Sun, Sand and Sea: The Emergent Tourism Programme in the Turks and Caicos Islands', *Journal of Heritage Tourism*, 3(1), pp. 55–73.

Chang, T. C. (1999) 'Local Uniqueness in the Global Village: Heritage Tourism in Singapore', *The Professional Geographer*, 51(1), pp. 91–103.

Cohen, E. (1985) 'The Tourist Guide: The Origins, Structure and Dynamics of a Role', *Annals of Tourism Research*, 12(1), pp. 5–29.

Cohen, E. (1988) 'Authenticity and Commoditization in Tourism', *Annals of Tourism Research*, 15(3), pp. 371–86.

Cohen, E., and Cohen, S. A. (2012) 'Current Sociological Theories and Issues in Tourism', *Annals of Tourism Research*, 39(4), pp. 2177–2202.

Coles, T., and Church, A. (2007). 'Tourism, Politics and the Forgotten Entanglements of Power', in Church, A., and Coles, T. (eds.), *Tourism, Power and Space*. London: Routledge, pp. 1–42.

Colley, S. (2015) 'Ethics and Digital Heritage', in Ireland, T., and Schofield, J. (eds.) *The Ethics of Cultural Heritage*. New York: Springer, pp. 13–32.

Corsane, G., Davis, P., Elliot, S., Maggi, M., Murtas, D. and Rogers, S. (2007) 'Ecomuseum Evaluation: Experiences in Piemonte and Liguria, Italy', *International Journal of Heritage Studies*, 13(2), pp. 101–16.

Craik, J. (1994) 'Peripheral Pleasures: The Peculiarities of Post-colonial Tourism', *Culture and Policy*, 6(1), pp. 21–31.

Crang, M. (1997) 'Picturing Practices: Research through the Tourist Gaze', *Progress in Human Geography*, 21(3), pp. 359–73.

Davis, P. (2004) 'Ecomuseums and the Democratisation of Japanese Museology', *International Journal of Heritage Studies*, 10(1), pp. 93–110.

Davis, P. (2007) 'Ecomuseums and Sustainability in Italy, Japan and China: Concept Adaptation through Implementation', in Knell, S., MacLeod, S. and Watson, S. (eds.), *Museum Revolutions: How Museums Change and Are Changed*. Routledge, pp. 198–214.

Davis, P. (2008) 'New Museologies and the Ecomuseum', in Graham, B., and Howard, P. (eds.), *The Ashgate Research Companion to Heritage and Identity*. Aldershot: Ashgate, pp. 397–414.

Doorne, S., Ateljevic, I. and Bai, Z. (2003) 'Representing Identities through Tourism: Encounters of Ethnic Minorities in Dali, Yunnan Province, People's Republic of China', *International Journal of Tourism Research*, 5(1), pp. 1–11.

Drost, A. (1996) 'Developing Sustainable Tourism for World Heritage Sites', *Annals of Tourism Research*, 23(2), pp. 479–84.

Van Eeden, J. (2004) 'The Colonial Gaze: Imperialism, Myths, and South African Popular Culture', *Design Issues*, 20(2), pp. 18–33.

Esfehani, M. H., and Albrecht, J. N. (2018) 'Roles of Intangible Cultural Heritage in Tourism in Natural Protected Areas', *Journal of Heritage Tourism*, 13(1), pp. 15–29.

Evans, G. (2004) 'Mundo Maya: From Cancún to City of Culture. World Heritage in Post-colonial Mesoamerica', *Current Issues in Tourism*, 7(4–5), pp. 315–29.

Foucault, M. (1982) 'The Subject and Power', *Critical inquiry*, 8(4), pp. 777–95.

Franklin, A. (2003) *Tourism: An Introduction*. London;Thousand Oaks, CA; New Delhi: Sage.

Fraser, N. (2001) 'Social Justice in the Knowledge Society: Redistribution, Recognition, and Participation', in *Gut zu Wissen Conference Papers*. Heinrich Böll Stiftung, pp. 1–13.

Fraser, N. (2003) 'Social Justice in the Age of Identity Politics: Distribution, Recognition, and Participation', in Honneth, A., and Fraser, N. (eds.), *Redistribution or Recognition? A Political-Philosophical Exchange*. London; New York: Verso, pp. 7–109.

Gan, D. (2009) 'The Paradox of Eco-museum Chinalization', *Journal of Minzu University of China (Philosophy and Social Sciences Edition)*, 36(2), pp. 68–73.

Garrod, B., and Fyall, A. (2001) 'Heritage Tourism: A Question of Definition', *Annals of Tourism Research*, 28(4), pp. 1049–52.

Gellner, E. (1983) *Nations and Nationalism*. Ithaca, NY: Cornell University Press.

Gmelch, G. (2003) *Behind the Smile: The Working Lives of Caribbean Tourism*. Bloomington: Indiana University Press.

Graburn, N. (1983). 'The Anthropology of Tourism', *Annals of Tourism Research*, 10(1), pp. 9–33.

Graburn, N. (2004) 'Authentic Inuit Art: Creation and Exclusion in the Canadian North', *Journal of Material Culture*, 9(2), pp. 141–59.

Graburn, N. (2015) 'Ethnic Tourism in Rural China: Cultural or Economic Development?', in Diekmann, A., and Smith, M. K. (eds.), *Ethnic and Minority Cultures As Tourist Attractions*. Bristol: Channel View Publications, pp. 176–87.

Graburn, N. (2018) 'Epilogue: Indigeneity, Researchers, and Tourism', in Bunten, A. C., and Graburn, N. H. H. (eds.), *Indigenous Tourism Movements*. Toronto; Buffalo: University of Toronto Press, pp. 242–58.

Graburn, N., and Jin,L. (2017) 'Tourism and Museums in China', *Asian Journal of Tourism Research* 2(1), pp. 1–35.

Gramsci, A. (1971) *Selections from the Prison Notebooks of Antonio Gramsci*. New York: International Publishers.

Gray, B. (1989) *Collaborating: Finding Common Ground for Multiparty Problems.* 1st ed. Jossey-Bass Management Series.San Francisco: Jossey-Bass.

Greenwood, D. J. (1989) 'Culture by the Pound: An Anthropological Perspective on Tourism As Cultural Commoditization', in Smith, V. L. (ed.), *Hosts and Guests.* Philadelphia: University of Pennsylvania Press, pp. 171–86.

Hafstein, V. T. (2004) 'The Politics of Origins: Collective Creation Revisited', *Journal of American Folklore*, 117(465), pp. 300–15.

Hafstein, V. T. (ed.) (2009) 'Intangible Heritage As a List: From Masterpieces to Representation', in Smith, Laurajane and Akagawa, Natsuko (eds.), *Intangible Heritage.* Key Issues in Intangible Heritage. London; New York: Routledge, pp. 93–111.

Hall, C. M. (2013) 'Framing Tourism Geography: Notes from the Underground', *Annals of Tourism Research*, 43, pp. 601–23.

Hall, S. (1999) 'Un-settling "the Heritage", Re-imagining the Post-nation: Whose Heritage?', *Third Text*, 13(49), pp. 3–13.

Handler, R. (1988) *Nationalism and the Politics of Culture in Quebec.* Madison: University of Wisconsin Press.

Harrison, D. (1992) 'Tourism to Less Developed Countries: The Social Consequences', in Harrison, D. (ed.), *Tourism and the Less Developed Countries.* London: Belhaven, pp. 19–34.

Harrison, D. (2001) 'Tourism to Less Developed Countries: Key Issues.', in Harrison, D. (ed.), *Tourism and the Less Developed Countries: Issues and Case Studies.* New York: Cabi, pp. 23–46.

Harrison, R. (2010) 'What Is Heritage?', in Harrison, R. (ed.), *Understanding the Politics of Heritage.* Manchester: Manchester University Press in association with the Open University, pp. 5–42.

Harrison, R. (2013) *Heritage: Critical Approaches.* Milton Park, Abingdon; New York: Routledge.

Harrison, R., and Hughes, L. (2010) 'Heritage, Colonialism and Postcolonialism', in Harrison, R. (ed.), *Understanding the Politics of Heritage.* Manchester: Manchester University Press in association with the Open University, pp. 234–69.

Harvey, D. (2001) 'Heritage Pasts and Heritage Presents: Temporality, Meaning and the Scope of Heritage Studies', *International Journal of Heritage Studies*, 7(4), pp. 319–38.

Harvey, D. (2004) 'The "New" Imperialism: Accumulation by Dispossession', *Socialist Register*, 40, pp. 63–87.

Harvey, D. (2008) 'The History of Heritage', in Graham, B. J., and Howard, P. (eds.), *The Ashgate Research Companion to Heritage and Identity*. Farnham: Ashgate, pp. 19–36.

d'Hauteserre, A.-M. (2006) 'Landscapes of the Tropics: Tourism and the New Cultural Economy in the Third World', in Terkenli, T. S., and d'Hauteserre, A.-M. (eds.), *Landscapes of a New Cultural Economy of Space*. Dordrecht: Springer, pp. 149–69.

Henderson, J. C. (2002) 'Tourism and Politics in the Korean Peninsula', *Journal of Tourism Studies*, 13(2), p. 16–27.

Henderson, J. C. (2007) 'Communism, Heritage and Tourism in East Asia', *International Journal of Heritage Studies*, 13(3), pp. 240–54.

Herzfeld, M. (2004) *The Body Impolitic: Artisans and Artifice in the Global Hierarchy of Value*. Chicago: University of Chicago Press.

Herzfeld, M. (2006) 'Spatial Cleansing: Monumental Vacuity and the Idea of the West', *Journal of Material Culture*, 11(1–2), pp. 127–49.

Herzfeld, M. (2015) 'Heritage and the Right to the City: When Securing the Past Creates Insecurity in the Present', *Heritage & Society*, 8(1), pp. 3–23.

Hewison, R. (1987) *The Heritage Industry: Britain in a Climate of Decline*. London: Methuen.

Hewison, R. (1989) 'Heritage: An Interpretation', in Uzzell, D. L. (ed.), *Heritage Interpretation: The Natural and Built Environment*. London: Belhaven Press, pp. 15–24.

Higgins-Desbiolles, F. (2016) 'Sustaining Spirit: A Review and Analysis of an Urban Indigenous Australian Cultural Festival', *Journal of Sustainable Tourism*, 24(8–9), pp. 1280–97.

Hobsbawm, E. J., and Ranger, T. O. (eds.) (1983) *The Invention of Tradition*. Past and Present Publications. Cambridge [Cambridgeshire]; New York: Cambridge University Press .

Hollinshead, K. (1992) '"White" Gaze, "Red" People – Shadow Visions: The Disidentification of "Indians" in Cultural Tourism', *Leisure Studies*, 11(1), pp. 43–64.

Holtorf, C. (2015) 'Averting Loss Aversion in Cultural Heritage', *International Journal of Heritage Studies*, 21(4), pp. 405–21.

Holtorf, C. (2018) 'Embracing Change: How Cultural Resilience Is Increased through Cultural Heritage', *World Archaeology*, 50(4), pp. 639–50.

Hom, S. M. (2015) *The Beautiful Country: Tourism and the Impossible State of Destination Italy*. Toronto: University of Toronto Press.

Howard, P. (2002) 'The Eco-museum: Innovation That Risks the Future', *International Journal of Heritage Studies*, 8(1), pp. 63–72.

Io, M.-U. (2013) 'Testing a Model of Effective Interpretation to Boost the Heritage Tourism Experience: A Case Study in Macao', *Journal of Sustainable Tourism*, 21(6), pp. 900–14.

Iorio, M., and Corsale, A. (2013) 'Diaspora and Tourism: Transylvanian Saxons Visiting the Homeland', *Tourism Geographies*, 15(2), pp. 198–232.

Jamal, T. (2019) *Justice and Ethics in Tourism*. Abingdon, Oxon; New York: Routledge.

de Jong, F. (2016) 'A Masterpiece of Masquerading: Contradictions of Conservation in Intangible Heritage', in de Jong, F., and Rowlands, M. (eds.), *Reclaiming Heritage*. 1st edn. Routledge, pp. 161–84.

Jordan, L.-A., and Jolliffe, L. (2013) 'Heritage Tourism in the Caribbean: Current Themes and Challenges', *Journal of Heritage Tourism*, 8(1), pp. 1–8.

Kirshenblatt-Gimblett, B. (1998) *Destination Culture: Tourism, Museums, and Heritage*. Berkeley: University of California Press.

Kurin, R. (2004) 'Safeguarding Intangible Cultural Heritage in the 2003 UNESCO Convention: A Critical Appraisal', *Museum International*, 56(1–2), pp. 66–77.

Lähdesmäki, T., Thomas, S. and Zhu, Y. (eds.) (2019) *Politics of Scale: New Directions in Critical Heritage Studies*. New York: Berghahn Books.

Laverack, G., and Wallerstein, N. (2001) 'Measuring Community Empowerment: A Fresh Look at Organizational Domains', *Health Promotion International*, 16(2), pp. 179–85.

Leask, A., and Fyall, A. (eds.) (2006) *Managing World Heritage Sites*. Oxford: Butterworth-Heinemann.

Leiper, N. (1979) 'The Framework of Tourism: Towards a Definition of Tourism, Tourist, and the Tourist Industry', *Annals of Tourism Research*, 6(4), pp. 390–407.

Lewis, P. (1979) 'Axioms for Reading the Landscape: Some Guides to the American Scene'. In Meinig, D. (ed.), *The Interpretation of Ordinary Landscapes*. New York: Oxford University Press, pp. 11–32.

Li, Y., Hu, Z. Y. and Zhang, C. Z. (2010) 'Red Tourism: Sustaining Communist Identity in a Rapidly Changing China', *Journal of Tourism and Cultural Change*, 8(1–2), pp. 101–19.

Light, D. (2000) 'Gazing on Communism: Heritage Tourism and Post-communist Identities in Germany, Hungary and Romania', *Tourism Geographies*, 2(2), pp. 157–76.

Light, D. (2015) 'Heritage and Tourism', in Waterton, E., and Watson, S. (eds.), *The Palgrave Handbook of Contemporary Heritage Research*. London: Palgrave Macmillan UK, pp. 144–58.

Logan, W. S., and Reeves, K. (eds.) (2009) *Places of Pain and Shame: Dealing with 'Difficult Heritage'*. Key Issues in Cultural Heritage. London: Routledge.

Lowenthal, D. (2015) *The Past Is a Foreign Country Revisited*. New York: Cambridge University Press.

Lyons, M., Smuts, C. and Stephens, A. (2001) 'Participation, Empowerment and Sustainability:(How) Do the Links Work?', *Urban Studies*, 38(8), pp. 1233–51.

MacCannell, D. (1976) *The Tourist: A New Theory of the Leisure Class*. New York: Schocken Books.

Macdonald, S. (2006) 'Mediating Heritage: Tour Guides at the Former Nazi Party Rally Grounds, Nuremberg', *Tourist Studies*, 6(2), pp. 119–38.

Macdonald, S. (2013) *Memorylands: Heritage and Identity in Europe Today*. London;New York: Routledge.

Macdonald, S. (2015) 'Is "Difficult Heritage" Still "Difficult"? Why Public Acknowledgment of Past Perpetration May No Longer Be so Unsettling to Collective Identities', *Museum International*, 67(1–4), pp. 6–22.

Marschall, S. (2009) *Landscape of Memory: Commemorative Monuments, Memorials and Public Statuary in Post-apartheid South Africa*. Leiden; Boston: Brill.

McIntosh, A. J., and Prentice, R. C. (1999) 'Affirming Authenticity: Consuming Cultural Heritage', *Annals of Tourism Research*, 26(3), pp. 589–612.

Meskell, L. (2019) 'Heritage, Gentrification, Participation: Remaking Urban Landscapes in the Name of Culture and Historic Preservation', *International Journal of Heritage Studies*, 25(9), pp. 996–8.

Modlin Jr, E. A., Alderman, D. H. and Gentry, G. W. (2011) 'Tour Guides As Creators of Empathy: The Role of Affective Inequality in Marginalizing the Enslaved at Plantation House Museums', *Tourist Studies*, 11(1), pp. 3–19.

Mookherjee, N. (2011) 'The Aesthetics of Nations: Anthropological and Historical Approaches', *Journal of the Royal Anthropological Institute*, 17, pp. 1–20.

Morgan, N., Pritchard, A., Causevic, S. and Minnaert, L. (2018) 'Ten Years of Critical Tourism Studies: Reflections on the Road Less Traveled', *Tourism Analysis*, 23(2), pp. 183–7.

Moscardo, G. (1996) 'Mindful Visitors: Heritage and Tourism', *Annals of Tourism Research*, 23(2), pp. 376–97.

Moscardo, G. (2011) 'Exploring Social Representations of Tourism Planning: Issues for Governance', *Journal of Sustainable Tourism*, 19(4–5), pp. 423–36.

Mosedale, J. (2006) 'Tourism Commodity Chains: Market Entry and Its Effects on St Lucia', *Current Issues in Tourism*, 9(4–5), pp. 436–58.

Mosedale, J. (2010) *Political Economy and Tourism: A Critical Perspective.* London: Routledge.

Nagaoka, M. (2015) '"European" and "Asian" Approaches to Cultural Landscapes Management at Borobudur, Indonesia in the 1970s', *International Journal of Heritage Studies*, 21(3), pp. 232–49.

Nakano, R., and Zhu, Y. (2020). 'Heritage As Soft Power: Japan and China in International Politics', *International Journal of Cultural Policy*, 26(7), 869–81.

Nash, D. (1978) 'Tourism As a Form of Imperialism', in Smith, V. L. (ed.), *Hosts and Guests: The Anthropology of Tourism.* Oxford: Basil Blackwell, pp. 37–52.

Nash, D. (1989) 'Tourism As a Form of Imperialism', in Smith, V. L. (ed.), *Hosts and Guests: The Anthropology of Tourism.* Second edition. Philadelphia: University of Pennsylvania Press, pp. 37–52.

Niewiadomski, P. (2020) 'COVID-19: From Temporary De-globalisation to a Re-discovery of Tourism?', *Tourism Geographies*, 22(3), pp. 1–6.

Nitzky, W. (2012) 'Mediating Heritage Preservation and Rural Development: Ecomuseum Development in China', *Urban Anthropology and Studies of Cultural Systems and World Economic Development*, 41(2/3/4), pp. 367–417.

Nora, P. (1989) 'Between Memory and History: *Les lieux de mémoire*', *Representations*, 26, pp. 7–24.

Notar, B. E. (2006) *Displacing Desire: Travel and Popular Culture in China.* Honolulu: University of Hawai'i Press.

Nuñez, T. A. (1963) 'Tourism, Tradition, and Acculturation: *Weekendismo* in a Mexican Village', *Ethnology*, 2(3), pp. 347–52.

Nuryanti, W. (1996) 'Heritage and Postmodern Tourism', *Annals of Tourism Research*, 23(2), pp. 249–60.

Nyíri, P. (2006) *Scenic Spots: Chinese Tourism, the State, and Cultural Authority.* Seattle: University of Washington Press.

Oakes, T. S. (1993) 'The Cultural Space of Modernity: Ethnic Tourism and Place Identity in China', *Environment and Planning D: Society and Space*, 11(1), pp. 47–66.

Palmer, C. (1998) 'From Theory to Practice: Experiencing the Nation in Everyday Life', *Journal of Material Culture*, 3(2), pp. 175–99.

Palmer, C., and Tivers, J. (eds.) (2019). *Creating Heritage for Tourism.* London; New York: Routledge.

Pedwell, C. (2012) 'Affective (self-) Transformations: Empathy, Neoliberalism and International Development', *Feminist Theory*, 13(2), pp. 163–79.

Perrons, D. (1999) 'Reintegrating Production and Consumption, or Why Political Economy Still Matters', in Munck, R., and O'Hearn, D. (eds.),

Critical Development Theory: Contributions to a New Paradigm. London: Zed Books, pp. 91–112.

Poria, Y., Biran, A. and Reichel, A. (2009) 'Visitors' Preferences for Interpretation at Heritage Sites', *Journal of Travel Research*, 48(1), pp. 92–105.

Porter, B. W., and Salazar, N. B. (2005) 'Heritage Tourism, Conflict, and the Public Interest: An Introduction', *International Journal of Heritage Studies*, 11(5), pp. 361–70.

Pretes, M. (2003) 'Tourism and Nationalism', *Annals of Tourism Research*, 30(1), pp. 125–42.

Pritchard, A., and Morgan, N. (2007) 'De-centring Tourism's Intellectual Universe, or Traversing the Dialogue between Change and Tradition', in Ateljevic, I., Pritchard, A. and Morgan, N. (eds.), *The Critical Turn in Tourism Studies*. Amsterdam: Elsevier, pp. 11–28.

Reisinger, Y., and Steiner, C. (2006) 'Reconceptualising Interpretation: The Role of Tour Guides in Authentic Tourism', *Current Issues in Tourism*, 9(6), pp. 481–98.

Richards, G. (2007) 'Culture and Authenticity in a Traditional Event: The Views of Producers, Residents, and Visitors in Barcelona', *Event Management*, 11(1–2), pp. 33–44.

Rico, T. (2016) *Constructing Destruction: Heritage Narratives in the Tsunami City*. London;New York: Routledge.

Ross, M. (2015) 'Interpreting the New Museology', *Museum and Society*, 2(2), pp. 84–103.

Rössler, M. (1995) 'UNESCO and Cultural Landscape Protection.' In B. von Droste, H. Plachter and M. Rössler (eds.), *Cultural Landscapes of Universal Value: Components of a Global Strategy*. Jena: Gustav Fischer in cooperation with UNESCO, pp.42–9.

Said, E. W. (1978) *Orientalism*. New York: Pantheon Books.

Said, E. W. (1993) *Culture and Imperialism*. New York: Vintage Books (Random House).

Saito, H. (2016) *The History Problem: The Politics of War Commemoration in East Asia*. Honolulu: University of Hawai'i Press.

Salazar, N. B. (2010) 'The Glocalisation of Heritage through Tourism', in Labadi, S., and Long, C. (eds.), *Heritage and Globalisation*. London: Routledge, pp. 131–45.

Salazar, N. B., and Zhu, Y. (2015) 'Heritage and Tourism', in Meskell, L. (ed.), *Global Heritage: A Reader*. Chichester: Wiley Blackwell, pp. 240–58.

Samuel, R. (1994) *Theatres of Memory: Past and Present in Contemporary Culture*. London; New York: Verso.

Sang, Y. (2009) '1979: Huang Shan, Selling Scenery to the Bourgeoisie: An Oral History Account of Chinese Tourism, 1949–1979', *China Heritage Quarterly*, 18, n.p.

Schein, L. (1997) 'Gender and Internal Orientalism in China', *Modern China*, 23(1), pp. 69–98.

Scherle, N., and Nonnenmann, A. (2008) 'Swimming in Cultural Flows: Conceptualising Tour Guides As Intercultural Mediators and Cosmopolitans', *Journal of Tourism and Cultural Change*, 6(2), pp. 120–37.

Schmitt, T. M. (2008) 'The UNESCO Concept of Safeguarding Intangible Cultural Heritage: Its Background and *Marrakchi* Roots', *International Journal of Heritage Studies*, 14(2), pp. 95–111.

Schofield, J. (ed.) (2016) *Who Needs Experts? Counter-mapping Cultural Heritage*. London; New York: Routledge.

Seaton, A. V. (2001) 'Sources of Slavery – Destinations of Slavery: The Silences and Disclosures of Slavery Heritage in the UK and US', *International Journal of Hospitality & Tourism Administration*, 2(3–4), pp. 107–29.

Shackley, M. (2004) 'Tourist Consumption of Sacred Landscapes Space, Time and Vision', *Tourism Recreation Research*, 29(1), pp. 67–73.

Shumway, N. (1991) *The Invention of Argentina*. Berkeley, Los Angeles and London: University of California Press.

Silberman, N. A. (2012) 'Heritage Interpretation and Human Rights: Documenting Diversity, Expressing Identity, or Establishing Universal Principles?', *International Journal of Heritage Studies*, 18(3), pp. 245–56.

Simpson, L., Wood, L. and Daws, L. (2003) 'Community Capacity Building: Starting with People not Projects', *Community Development Journal*, 38(4), pp. 277–86.

Sinclair-Maragh, G., and Gursoy, D. (2015) 'Imperialism and Tourism: The Case of Developing Island Countries', *Annals of Tourism Research*, 50, pp. 143–58.

Skounti, A. (2009) 'The Authentic Illusion: Humanity's Intangible Cultural Heritage, the Moroccan Experience', in Smith, L., and Akagawa, N. (eds.), *Intangible Heritage*. London; New York: Routledge, pp. 74–92.

Smith, L. (2006) *Uses of Heritage*. London;New York: Routledge.

Smith, L., and Akagawa, N. (eds.) (2009) *Intangible Heritage*. London; New York: Routledge.

Smith, L., Wetherell, M. and Campbell, G. (eds.). (2018). *Emotion, Affective Practices, and the Past in the Present*. London; New York: Routledge.

Sodaro, A. (2011) 'Politics of the Past: Remembering the Rwandan Genocide at the Kigali Memorial Centre', in Lehrer, E., Milton, C. E. and Patterson, M. E. (eds.), *Curating Difficult Knowledge*. Basingstoke: Palgrave Macmillan, pp. 72–88.

Sofield, T. H., and Li, F. M. S. (1998) 'Tourism Development and Cultural Policies in China', *Annals of Tourism Research*, 25(2), pp. 362–92.

Staiff, R. (2016) *Re-imagining Heritage Interpretation: Enchanting the Past-Future*. London; New York: Routledge.

Steiner, L., and Frey, B. S. (2012) 'Correcting the Imbalance of the World Heritage List: Did the UNESCO Strategy Work?', *Journal of International Organizations Studies*, 3(1), pp. 25–40.

Stovel, H. (2005) 'Introduction', in Stovel, H., Stanley-Price, N. and Killick, R. (eds.), *Conservation of Living Religious Heritage*. Rome: ICCROM Conservation Studies, pp. 1–11.

Theodossopoulos, D. (2013) 'Emberá Indigenous Tourism and the Trap of Authenticity: Beyond Inauthenticity and Invention', *Anthropological Quarterly*, 86(2), pp. 397–425.

Theodossopoulos, D. (2018) 'Indigenous Tourism As a Transformative Process: The Case of the Emberá in Panama', in Bunten, A. C., and Graburn, N. H. H. (eds.), *Indigenous Tourism Movements*. Toronto; Buffalo: University of Toronto Press, pp. 99–116.

Timothy, D. J. (1999) 'Participatory Planning: A view of Tourism in Indonesia', *Annals of Tourism Research*, 26(2), pp. 371–91.

Timothy, D. J. (2007) 'Empowerment and Stakeholder Participation in Tourism Destination Communities', in Church, A., and Coles, T. (eds.), *Tourism, Power and Space*. London: Routledge, pp. 199–216.

Timothy, D. J. (2011) *Cultural Heritage and Tourism: An Introduction*. Bristol; Buffalo; Toronto: Channel View Publications.

Timothy, D. J., and Boyd, S. W. (2003) *Heritage Tourism*. Harlow: Prentice Hall.

Timothy, D. J., and Boyd, S. W. (2006) 'Heritage Tourism in the 21st Century: Valued Traditions and New Perspectives', *Journal of Heritage Tourism*, 1(1), pp. 1–16.

Timothy, D. J., and Tosun, C. (2003) 'Appropriate Planning for Tourism in Destination Communities: Participation, Incremental Growth and Collaboration', in *Tourism in Destination Communities*. Cabi, pp. 181–204.

Tomlinson, J. (1991) *Cultural Imperialism: A Critical Introduction*. Baltimore, MD: Johns Hopkins University Press.

Towner, J. (1985) 'The Grand Tour: A Key Phase in the History of Tourism', *Annals of Tourism Research*, 12(3), pp. 297–333.

Tribe, J. (2007) 'Critical Tourism: Rules and Resistance', in In Ateljevic, I., Morgan, N. and Pritchard, A. (eds.), *The Critical Turn in Tourism Studies: Innovative Research Methodologies*. Oxford: Elsevier, pp. 29–40.

Tribe, J. (2008) 'Tourism: A Critical Business', *Journal of Travel Research*, 46(3), pp. 245–55.

Tucker, H. (2016) 'Empathy and Tourism: Limits and Possibilities', *Annals of Tourism Research*, 57, pp. 31–43.

Tunbridge, J. E., and Ashworth, G. J. (1996) *Dissonant Heritage: The Management of the Past As a Resource in Conflict*. Chichester: John Wiley & Sons.

Turner, P., Turner, S. and Carroll, F. (2005) 'The Tourist Gaze: Towards Contextualised Virtual Environments', in Turner P., and Davenport E. (eds.), *Spaces, Spatiality and Technology*. Heidelberg: Springer, pp. 281–97.

UNESCO (1992) 'Operational Guidelines for the Implementation of the World Heritage Convention'. Available at: http://whc.unesco.org/archive/out/guide92.htm.

UNESCO (2003) 'Text of the Convention for the Safeguarding of the Intangible Cultural Heritage'. Available at: https://ich.unesco.org/en/convention.

UNESCO (2019) *Operational Guidelines for the Implementation of the World Heritage Convention*. Paris: World Heritage Centre.

UNWTO (2008) Glossary of Tourism Terms. From www.unwto.org/glossary-tourism-terms#:~:text=Tourism%20is%20a%20social%2C%20cultural,personal%20or%20business%2Fprofessional%20purposes.

UNWTO (2018) *UNWTO Tourism Highlights: 2018Edition*. Madrid: UNWTO.

Urry, J. (1990) *The Tourist Gaze: Leisure and Travel in Contemporary Societies (Theory, Culture & Society)*. Thousand Oaks, CA: Sage.

Vecco, M. (2010) 'A Definition of Cultural Heritage: From the Tangible to the Intangible', *Journal of Cultural Heritage*, 11(3), pp. 321–4.

Wang, N. (1999) 'Rethinking Authenticity in Tourism Experience', *Annals of Tourism Research*, 26(2), pp. 349–70.

Waterton, E., and Smith, L. (2010) 'The Recognition and Misrecognition of Community Heritage', *International Journal of Heritage Studies*, 16(1–2), pp. 4–15.

Wergin, C. (2012) 'Trumping the Ethnic Card: How Tourism Entrepreneurs on Rodrigues Tackled the 2008 Financial Crisis', *Island Studies Journal*, 7(1), pp. 119–34.

Wergin, C. (2016) 'Dreamings beyond "Opportunity": The Collaborative Economics of an Aboriginal Heritage Trail', *Journal of Cultural Economy*, 9(5), pp. 488–506.

Wilson, M., Ballard, C. and Kalotiti, D. (2011) 'Chief Roi Mata's Domain: Challenges for a World Heritage Property in Vanuatu', *Historic Environment*, 23(2), pp. 5–11.

Wilson, M., Ballard, C., Matanik, R. and Warry T. (2012) *Community As the First C: Conservation and Development through Tourism at Chief Roi Mata's Domain, Vanuatu*. Paris: United Nations Educational, Scientific and Cultural Organization (UNESCO).

Winter, T. (2009) 'The Modernities of Heritage and Tourism: Interpretations of an Asian Future', *Journal of Heritage Tourism*, 4(2), pp. 105–15.

Winter, T. (2014) 'Heritage Studies and the Privileging of Theory', *International Journal of Heritage Studies*, 20(5), pp. 556–72.

Wollentz, G. (2017) 'Making a Home in Mostar: Heritage and the Temporalities of Belonging', *International Journal of Heritage Studies*, 23(10), pp. 928–45.

Wood, R. E. (1984) 'Ethnic Tourism, the State, and Cultural Change in Southeast Asia', *Annals of Tourism Research*, 11(3), pp. 353–74.

Wood, R. E. (1997) 'Tourism and the State: Ethnic Options and Constructions of Otherness', in Picard, M., and Wood, R. E. (eds.), *Tourism, Ethnicity, and the State in Asian and Pacific Societies*. Honolulu: University of Hawai'i Press, pp. 1–34.

Wright, P. (2009) *On Living in an Old Country: The National Past in Contemporary Britain*. Oxford: Oxford University Press.

Xiao, H., Jafari, J., Cloke, P. and Tribe, J. (2013) 'Annals: 40–40 Vision', *Annals of Tourism Research*, 40(1), pp. 352–85.

Young, I. M. (1990) *Justice and the Politics of Difference*. Princeton, NJ: Princeton University Press.

Zeppel, H., and Muloin, S. (2008) 'Aboriginal Interpretation in Australian Wildlife Tourism', *Journal of Ecotourism*, 7(2–3), pp. 116–36.

Zhu, Y. (2012) 'Performing Heritage: Rethinking Authenticity in Tourism', *Annals of Tourism Research*, 39(3), pp. 1495–1513.

Zhu, Y. (2015) 'Cultural Effects of Authenticity: Contested Heritage Practices in China', *International Journal of Heritage Studies*, 21(6), pp. 594–608.

Zhu, Y. (2018a) *Heritage and Romantic Consumption in China*. Amsterdam: Amsterdam University Press.

Zhu, Y. (2018b) 'Lifestyle Mobility: Shifting Conception of Home in Modern China', *International Journal of Tourism Anthropology*, 6(4), 357–374.

Zhu, Y. (2020) 'Memory, Homecoming and the Politics of Diaspora Tourism in China', *Tourism Geographies*, 1–18.

Zhu, Y., Jin, L. and Graburn, N. (2017). 'Domesticating Tourism Anthropology in China', *American Anthropologist*, 119(4), 730–5.

Zhu, Y., and Maags, C. (2020) *Heritage Politics in China: The Power of the Past*. New York: Routledge.

Zwigenberg, R. (2014) *Hiroshima: The Origins of Global Memory Culture*. Cambridge: Cambridge University Press.

Cambridge Elements ≡

Critical Heritage Studies

Kristian Kristiansen
University of Gothenburg

Michael Rowlands
UCL

Francis Nyamnjoh
University of Cape Town

Astrid Swenson
Bath University

Shu-Li Wang
Academia Sinica

Ola Wetterberg
University of Gothenburg

About the Series

This series focuses on the recently established field of Critical Heritage Studies. Interdisciplinary in character, it brings together contributions from experts working in a range of fields, including cultural management, anthropology, archaeology, politics, and law. The series will include volumes that demonstrate the impact of contemporary theoretical discourses on heritage found throughout the world, raising awareness of the acute relevance of critically analysing and understanding the way heritage is used today to form new futures.

Cambridge Elements ≡

Critical Heritage Studies

Printed in the United States
by Baker & Taylor Publisher Services